ach

The dea
Negotiati   :h is exactly
what a hi   lesperson's job
is to brin;   ble and ultimately fo   ion. They do
whatever   iting this way
usually overpay and never know it.

The hassle free approach

Top Secrets Revealed walks you through a proven step-by-step
method used by the author. You will be amazed how easy it is to
bypass salespeople and keep the dealer's hidden profit in your pocket,
not theirs!

Key points offered include:

- ➤ know which dealers have the car you want to maximize your
  negotiating edge

- ➤ money saving secrets the dealer does not want you to know

- ➤ how to get a lower price on an already discounted car

- ➤ bypass the salesperson and be in complete control

- ➤ best times of year to buy

- ➤ buy vs. lease decision made easy

- ➤ calculating your trade-in value

- ➤ all your finance options

- ➤ the most comprehensive Internet research guide available

- ➤ best Online Car-Buying Services

This book treads where others dare not...

Within these pages are the deepest secrets *ever* told for getting the absolute lowest price possible - quickly, easily and completely sales pressure free.

"I couldn't believe it, the dealer gave me his lowest price immediately. I was amazed."
– Carol J., Sales Exec

"I'd recommend this book to anyone who dislikes the dealership buying experience."
– Fred R., Pilot

"Marc's information saved me from the salesperson but especially from myself."
– Doyle Barnette, Author

"I've read your lease chapter,
I FINALLY UNDERSTAND LEASING."
– Karen P., Interior Design

"I've bought lots of cars over the years but with this book, I was able to get the greatest deal ever."
– Ori Melamed, Exotic birds dealer

"This book led me to the best leasing bargain of my life and top dollar on my trade-in."
– Ken Cohen, Purveyor of fine coffee

"The wheel has been re-invented and this one flies."
– Robert C., Retired

Top Secrets Revealed

The Hassle Free Approach to Car Buying & Leasing

Top Secrets Revealed

The Hassle Free Approach to Car Buying & Leasing

Marc Vanasse

Quickread Publishing
Santa Barbara, California

Top Secrets Revealed: The Hassle Free Approach to Car Buying & Leasing. Copyright © 2004, Quickread Publishing. All rights reserved. Without prior permission in writing from the publisher, no part of this book may be reproduced or transmitted in any form or by any means. This includes mechanical, photocopying, electronic, recording or by any information storage or retrieval system. Short excerpts for use in published reviews are permitted.

The information in this book is based on years of successful transactions. Because every situation is unique, results may vary on your personal negotiations. The author and publisher assume no liability for the outcome of anyone's use of the strategies contained in this book. This book is not a rendering of legal advice or a representation of expert accounting principles. If legal, accounting or any expert advice is required, the author and publisher suggest that a legal or accounting professional be sought out.

Published by:
Quickread Publishing
P.O. Box 213
Santa Barbara, CA 93102

Publisher's Cataloging-in-Publication

Vanasse, Marc.
    Top secrets revealed : the hassle-free approach to
car buying & leasing / Marc Vanasse.
    p. cm.
    Includes index.
    LCCN 2004100510
    ISBN 0-9748947-0-2

    1. Automobiles--Purchasing. 2. Automobile leasing
and renting.   I. Title.

TL162.V363 2004   629.222'029
                         QBI04-200142

First Printing, 2004
First Edition

Gender Usage: This text is intended to be gender neutral.

Printed in the United States of America.
Cover design by Robert Wilmott
Cover photo by Mehosh Dziadzio
Interior design by Robert Wilmott, Linda Trujillo
Edited by Patrick Cunningham

For marketing, publicity or quantity discounts to promote products or services, send e-mail to a.sb@verizon.net

Dedication

To Robin for getting me started.

Contents at a Glance

Contents

12: Finalizing the Deal 107

About The Author

Marc Vanasse is an expert in every aspect of the car buying/leasing process. With over twenty years of experience, he has assisted hundreds of people in obtaining the car of their dreams at the absolute lowest price. He is respected among colleagues and clientele nationwide.

Author of two previous books:
- *How to Buy a Used Car Without Being Taken For a Ride!* © 1994
- *How to Sell Your Car and Get the Most For It!* © 1996

Acknowledgements

To the many who helped create this book, thank you. I have inadvertently lost track of some of you. Please accept my sincere apology and appreciation.

Among those closely involved were: Denise Homan, Brad McFadden, Anthony and Tony Carraccio, Michael Arick, Jenny Van Steyn, Sjoerd Koppert, Eric and Ilene Hancey, Jona Cole, Mark Collins and Lauren Tempkin.

Thanks also to: Elizabeth, Carol, Carolina, Tobias, Lisa, Judy, Debby, Larry, Danielle, Cheryl, Pat, Sharon, Chris, Dick, Jill, Susan, Dave, Lee, Katie, Stephanie, Richie, Fred, Elena, Donna, Greg, Joanne, Erin, John, Steve, Rob, Naomi, Fatima, Claudia, Dan, Penny, Lupita, Natalie and the countless coffee friends and Lazy Acres employees.

Thank you Michael Vance for the use of your beautiful Ford Thunderbird.

To Alex Livadas, a glaring exception and a pleasure to deal with.

To new car dealers: you're really good at what you do. I simply want to help the consumer.

1

What Type of Vehicle Do You Want?

In This Chapter

The first step in buying a new car is figuring out what is best for your lifestyle. If you have a family to drive around, a two seat convertible would be impractical. A large part of the decision making should be based on what you need and how much you can afford. If you are unsure of your needs, the following list should help you get on track:

1- Body Styles

- ✧ Small car
- ✧ Sports car
- ✧ Family sedan
- ✧ Luxury sedan
- ✧ Coupe
- ✧ Convertible
- ✧ Sport utility
- ✧ Pickup truck
- ✧ Minivan
- ✧ Station wagon
- ✧ Hatchback

2- Fuel Efficiency

- ✧ Electric
- ✧ Hybrid (gas and electric combination)

3- Comfort features

- ✧ Power windows
- ✧ Power seats
- ✧ Remote trunk release
- ✧ Premium sound
- ✧ Cup holders
- ✧ Premium wheels
- ✧ Glass sunroof
- ✧ Power sliding doors (minivans)
- ✧ Remote keyless entry and central locking
- ✧ Accessory controls on steering wheel
- ✧ Rear view mirrors that dim automatically

- ✧ Power mirrors
- ✧ Heated seats
- ✧ Cruise control
- ✧ Tilt steering
- ✧ Cargo net
- ✧ TV / Video
- ✧ CD

Defined:

- ✧ Sport suspension: *Gives a firmer ride for better control or high performance handling.*
- ✧ Navigation system: *Satellite based visual screen system to help guide you to your destination.*
- ✧ Telematics: *Subscription based services providing information or assistance from the vehicle.*
- ✧ Xenon Headlights: *High intensity bluish light system vastly improving night vision.*

4- Safety features

- ✧ Height adjustable seatbelts
- ✧ Alarm system
- ✧ Antilock brake system
- ✧ Side and head airbags
- ✧ Passenger-side air bag on/off switch

Defined:

- ✧ Electronic tire pressure monitor system: *Sensors provide tire air pressure information.*
- ✧ Parktronic: *Warning sensor alerts close proximity to an object.*
- ✧ Dual stage airbags: *Advanced computerized front air bags that deploy as needed.*
- ✧ Anti-whiplash headrest system: *Active computerized system that counters whiplash in an accident.*
- ✧ Brake assist: *Computer provides extra stopping power in an emergency.*
- ✧ Side skid control: *Computer controlled skid avoidance.*
- ✧ Traction control: *Computer controlled anti-wheel slippage.*
- ✧ Limited slip differential: *Distributes power to necessary drive wheel.*

☞ For more definitions on features, options or packages, go to www.cars.com, click on **News & Advice** then click on **Cars.com Glossary.**

5- Trim levels

An upgraded trim level will have more standard features in the base price of the car than a more modest trim level. For instance, the Honda Accord EX comes standard with a moon roof, leather interior and alloy wheels, while the lower grade trim level Honda Accord LX does not come standard with these features. These items would be considered options on an LX model and would add to the base price of the car.

6- Your Internet Connection

To learn more about trim levels available with the model you desire, check out the following websites or the manufacturer's website:

www.cars.com

www.carsdirect.com

www.jdpower.com
Click on **Automotive** then **Help me choose a new vehicle**

www.kbb.com (Kelley Blue Book website)

www.motortrendauto.com

A trip to the dealership can be very helpful in understanding how a car typically comes optioned and packaged from the manufacturer.

> ☞   Chapter 4, "How to Get On and Off the Car Lot Unscathed"
>   will guide you through the car lot experience.

♦ Rent a car, maybe even from a dealership. There's nothing like a lengthy test drive to help you decide if you want to buy it.

2

Researching Prices on Vehicles, Their Options and Packages

In This Chapter
1- Sources for Pricing Information
2- First Year's Ownership Costs

The window sticker price or *Manufacturer's Suggested Retail Price* (MSRP) includes the base price of the vehicle plus the options and packages (if any). Items that are standard equipment on the car are part of the base price. The window sticker price is pasted to one of the windows on the car.

A car typically comes optioned and packaged from the manufacturer a cetrtain way and is an important aspect you must know. Options (single items) and packages (groupings of two or more items) add to the base price of a vehicle because these items do not come as standard equipment. With this information you can make a distinct comparison between vehicles.

♦ Ask for the options and packages that add to the base price of the car then ask for the window sticker price.

If a vehicle typically comes packaged a certain way but you want it differently, your chances of finding that vehicle are greatly reduced.

For example, a Toyota Camry with side air bags may come with leather seats but will be much more difficult to find side airbags with cloth seats.

The following websites will be of great value in viewing current availability of specifications, packages, options and pricing:

STAR RATINGS: Website's have been given a star rating by the author with 5 stars being the top rating. Only 4 to 5 star ratings are listed.

1- Sources for Pricing Information

www.autobytel.com   4.3★
Click on **Research**, choose a "Make"

www.autosite.com   4.8★
Click on **Research**, choose a "Make"

www.autovantage.com   4.4★
Under "Car research", click on **New car summaries**

www.autoweb.com   4★
Under "Research", click on **New vehicles**

www.carpoint.com   4.8★
Choose a **Make** and **Model.** Clicking on an **option box** will update your total at bottom

www.carprices.com   4.5★
Click on **Research & price** then click on **Make**

www.cars.com   5★
Choose a "Make", "Model" enter "Zip code" and click on **Price with options**

www.carsdirect.com   5★
Select a **Make, Model** and click on **Go**

www.edmunds.com   4.8★
Click on **New cars**

www.kbb.com   4.5★
Click on **New car pricing**

www.motortrend.com   4.9★

The websites above are also Online Car Buying Services that can usually obtain a price for you below the window sticker price. These websites are not problem free.

☞   If the absolute lowest price is your main objective, see
Chapter 11, "Locate and Negotiate By Phone."

If you decide to buy or lease a car through one of these Online Car
Buying Services, a contact person from a local dealership will call you,
usually within twenty-four hours and ask, "When can you come in?"
Prepare yourself for this call. Read chapter 12.

☞   See Chapter 12, "Finalizing the Deal," and follow the
important guidelines. This chapter will show you how to keep
all further dealer profits in your pocket.

♦ **If you purchase or lease through an Online Car Buying Service,
you may pay a hidden fee through an increase in final price but
obtaining a quote is free and you don't have to buy.**

Auto Price Guides (available at your local library, bookstore or maga-
zine stand) are a great source for pricing information. In these guides, you
find dealer invoice and retail prices on most makes and models, including
their options and packages. You can find reviews by experts as well.

For expert reviews on most vehicles, go to the following websites:

☞   Future and concept cars are found in Chapter 14, the Internet
Directory, under item #40.

www.automobilemag.com   4★

www.carpoint.msn.com   4★
Click on **New Cars** then click on **Reviews**

www.cars.com   5★
Click on **All-New Models for 2005** (What's new for current year?)

www.caranddriver.com   4.5★

www.carsmart.com   4★
Under "Car Research", click on **Reviews**

www.edmunds.com   4.5★
Click on **Car Reviews**

www.motortrend.com   5★
Under "Road Tests", click on your "vehicle style"

For expert reviews on a new car test drive, go to the following websites:

New Car Test Drive
www.nctd.com   4.5★
Current and past test drive reviews

www.thecarconnection.com 4★
Click on **Reviews**

www.roadandtrack.com   5★

The following websites have information on future and concept cars:

www.kbb.com   5★
Under the heading "New Car Reviews & Ratings", click on
coming soon

www.edmunds.com   5★
Scroll to click on **Car Reviews** then click on **Concept Cars** or click
on **Future Vehicles**

www.motortrend.com   5★
Click on **future vehicles** (covers 1 to 4 future years)

2- First Year's Ownership Costs

Down Payment:
The amount of money you put down when you sign the contract. It's
usually 10 to 20 percent of the vehicle's cost. If you have great credit, it
can be less.

Monthly Loan Payment:
The amount of money you pay monthly toward your loan.
See "Loan Interest Table" in the Appendix to calculate your monthly
payment. Be sure to include any items that add to the price of the vehicle
such as: options, extended warranty and state fees.

State Fees:
Includes sales tax and license/registration fee. The dealership's finance
manager can tell you what these fees will be.

Finance Charge:
The interest rate on your car loan. The following websites will help you calculate your monthly loan payments quickly:

www.autovantage.com   5★
Click on **Car Research** then under "Finance Tools", click on **Loan Calculator**

www.autoweb.com   5★
Scroll to "Financing & Research" and click on **Auto Loan Calculator**

www.carpoint.msn.com   5★
On left side, click on **Finance**

www.eloan.com   5★
Click on **Auto Purchase** then on right side, click on **Rates and Payments**

Fuel:
The window sticker on the vehicle displays the approximate city and highway miles the vehicle gets per gallon of gas. Divide the amount of miles you drive per year by the miles per gallon stated on the window sticker to arrive at the number of gallons of gas you use per year. Take that number (gallons per year) and multiply it by the price of gas per gallon.

www.kbb.com
On home page click on **New car pricing** and follow the instructions to bring up the vehicle of choice. Scroll to the bottom of this page under **Engine specifications** to view fuel mileage estimates.

Insurance:
A fee to cover theft, collision, bodily injury and vandalism. Car insurance policies vary. You should get your insurance company to give you a price quote on the specific car you are interested in buying or leasing to make sure you can afford it. You can also get an insurance price quote at any of the following websites. Have your current policy available when viewing online sites.

www.autobytel.com
Click on **New** then scroll and click on **Insurance tools and research**

www.esurance.com
Enter "Zip Code", click **go** and fill-in a 5 minute form to get an instant quote

www.insure.com
Click on **Auto**

Maintenance:
The factory scheduled service to upkeep your car properly. Decide how many miles you drive per year, then call the dealership's service department and ask, "At what mileage intervals do I need factory scheduled services?" Your next question should be: "What are the prices of these services?" Make sure they include oil changes.

Depreciation:
The loss of value after you purchase your vehicle. This may be the greatest single cost of owning a new car. By looking at your local auto trader magazines and newspaper classified ads, you should get an idea of the new car's value in one year. Subtract the used car price from the new car price and the difference is the depreciation.

The following websites have classified listings for price comparisons. Look for similar one year old vehicles. The actual selling prices are usually lower. Dealer prices are typically higher than private party ads.

www.autotrader.com

www.cars.com

3

Best Times of Year to Buy

In This Chapter

Yes, there are certain times of the year that offer better price reductions than others. These special times are typically established by the manufacturer. The following are optimum times you can take advantage of in order to maximize your savings.

1- End of Sales Cycle

End of the month - The dealership may need to sell one more car in order to meet their sales goal, thereby allowing the car to be sold at a much lower price.

End of quarter (March, June, September and December) - A dealership that is about to meet their sales goal could allow you to buy at a very low price. Typically lower than end of the month prices.

End of model year - These are usually available in September or October when the next year model is about to come out. It's still a new car with full factory warranty and it's being sold at a discount. Find out when the new model year will show up in your area and buy the "end of model year" two weeks before to one week after the new ones show up.

Doing it in this time frame insures the dealer will more than likely still have a good selection in stock.

Advertised specials - The advertisement usually reads "1 at this price." These specials are great deals but beware the dealer may try to switch you if the car has already been sold. In these ads, there are usually one, two or three cars at a reduced price even though they may have a large inventory of the same car that's not on sale.

2- Manufacturer-to-Customer Rebates

A rebate is cash given to the customer by the manufacturer in order to boost car sales. It's their way of having a clearance sale. It can also be a low interest rate offer on a loan. Typically, the lower the interest rate offered, the shorter the loan term will be. Rebates are advertised in newspapers, radio and television ads. Some dealers may not tell you a rebate exists if you don't ask.

Normally you choose between a cash rebate or a low interest rate loan. It's rare they offer both but sometimes do.

To determine if a rebate exists:

> ➤ Watch and listen for media ads offering rebates

> ➤ Ask the dealer if there is a rebate on your model

> ➤ Go to the following websites for listings of current rebates

The independent websites below are updated according to their own schedules. Therefore, it's best that you go to every site to compile the most accurate information.

www.autobytel.com   4★
Click on **Research**

www.autopedia.com   4★
Scroll and click on **Consumer incentives and rebates**

www.autosite.com   5★
Click on **Research**

www.edmunds.com   5★
Click on **Incentives and Rebates**

www.intellichoice.com   4.5★
Scroll and click on **Rebates and Incentives**

www.kbb.com   5★

♦ If you are a recent college graduate or first-time buyer, you'll get an added discount if you meet the incentive criteria.

♦ If you are thinking of buying an end-of-year model for the savings you'll receive from the customer rebate, compare the two models thoroughly because the freshly new model may have features that will outweigh the financial savings of the previous model.

4

How To Get On and Off the Car Lot Unscathed

In This Chapter

1- Start Inside the Showroom

The dealership sales staff is highly trained at maximizing profit on each car sold. One of their key strategies is to get you inside the showroom after you have been out on the lot. This is their best opportunity to pressure you into buying or leasing with the whole sales team available. A signal from the salesperson will bring the sales manager, general manager or finance manager to join in on the pressure sell. They will play on your emotions and successful or not, attempt to pressure you into buying or leasing a car while most likely exhausting you in the process.

♦ If you follow the guidelines set forth in this book, you will get a lower price than what they offer at superstores, no dicker sticker or one-price shopping dealerships.

You can avoid all this sales pressure by going directly inside the showroom when you first arrive at the dealership and follow these three steps:

1. If you need a brochure, get it now. If the dealership doesn't have one, you can call another dealership later and have one mailed to you.

2. Most dealerships have a policy to photocopy your driver's license when you want to take a car for a test drive. Ask if this is their policy. If it is, give them your drivers license to photocopy but don't leave the showroom without it. Make sure you get your driver's license back. Keep in mind your license information may allow the dealer to call or write you.

3. Get the salesperson's business card BEFORE you leave the showroom. They usually don't carry business cards with them as a reason to get you back inside the showroom so the sales team will have a chance to pressure sell you.

♦ Luxury-make dealerships tend to have a lower sales pressure approach than volume-oriented dealerships.

♦ Occasionally, salespeople have been known to block in a customer's car as a sales pressure ploy. Parking for ease of departure can be invaluable.

♦ If you need to go to a dealership to gather information and get intimidated easily, bring a friend to keep you from an impulse buy. If you can't find someone to go with you, visit the lots before they open or after they close.

2- Top Sales Trick Questions and Answers to Guide You

The following are typical questions posed by sales people:

1. *"What will it take to get you into this car today?"*
Appease them by saying:
"I'm here to gather information so I can make an informed decision ."

2. *"What if I can get you a great deal on a* (specific car) *today?"*
"I'm not ready today, but thank you." Or: "My husband (wife, boyfriend, girlfriend) needs to approve the vehicle."
Otherwise, they will think you're a customer that is ready to buy.

3. *"What do I have to do to get you into a car today?"*
"I still need to look at various vehicles so I'm not ready to buy today."

4. *"When will you be ready to buy?"*
"Maybe in two or three weeks."
Don't let them think anytime sooner.

5. *"Will you be purchasing, financing, or leasing the vehicle?"*
"I don't know, I want to figure out my vehicle needs first."
This is an attempt to get you to commit to something—don't fall for it.

6. *"Are you trading-in your car?"*
"No."
It's best not to address a trade-in at this time.

7. *"What color do you like?"*
"I'm not sure, I would like to see the available colors."
If you tell the salesperson a specific color, it gives them a point of entry and they may start pushing for a sale.

8. *"Which other vehicles are you planning to look at?"*
"I would prefer to talk about the car you can show me, is that okay?"
Otherwise, they will tell you why their vehicle is better (biased of course).

9. *"What is your last name?"*
"For the sake of privacy, I would prefer not giving it out just yet."
If you give them your last name, they could look it up in the phone book and call you.

10. *"What is your phone number?"*
"I would prefer not to give it out at this time."
If you give out your real phone number, you will probably get several calls from salespeople later on. It's their job. If you feel you can't say no, give them a phone number immediately (real, obsolete or a fax number). Sometimes, because you're on their territory, it'll make it easier on yourself to give them a phone number.

11. *"Are you married?"*
    "Where do you work?"
    "What kind of work?"
    "What part of town do you live in?"
    "Have you lived in town long?"
    "What school do your kids go to?"

These questions are geared to your financial situation. It's generally best to hold back this type of information.

3- Sales Team Tricks

Once you've received all the information on a car that you want, the salesperson will usually turn up the sales pressure. A second sales team member may approach you and introduce themself, *"Hi, I'm Joe, what's your name?"* At this point, you should walk toward your car while saying, "Nice to meet you Joe, but I have to go." That is, unless you have nothing better to do for the next few hours. If you don't keep your feet moving in the direction of your car, you might drive off the lot with a new vehicle that you'll regret owning the next day.

As you are leaving, if you're asked, *"Did you have all your questions answered?"* Reply, "Yes, I did and I have your business card in case I have more questions. Thank you for your help." Keep walking.

The sales (tag) team works hard at getting you involved in negotiations. Once involved, they try to confuse you and wear you down so they can get more money from you. Don't give them a chance. There's no need to expose yourself to these time consuming tactics.

4- Watch for the Smoke and Mirrors

The following are typical lines used by salespeople:

➤ *"We're the only dealer with this car."*

➤ *"It's impossible to find this car."*

➤ *"There's a six-month waiting list for this car."*

➤ *"The car doesn't exist, you'll have to special order it with us."*
Chances are, if you call a few dealers you'll find several cars.

➤ *"No dealer will discount this model."* Although this may be the case, most dealers will discount any model. Call around to see for yourself.

➤ *"I will get you this vehicle for $X dollars."* (an unbelievably low price) As tempting as the offer may sound, do not counter it. This is a typical ploy to get you involved and into their office. Don't take the bait. The dealership isn't the place to negotiate any new car deal ever.

Keep in mind, you are at the dealership to gather information about the car only. Remind your salesperson of this fact. Do not discuss financing, leasing or any price other than the Manufacturer's Suggested Retail Price on the window. You could say, "I'm shopping around and I'm not yet sure which vehicle I want."

Warning: Do not sign any paperwork at this stage for any reason. If a writng instrument finds its way into your hand, put it down immediately. You could easily be fooled into giving the dealer permission to run your credit report which puts you at a serious negotiating disadvantage. You sign paperwork only once and that's *after* you completely finalize negotiations with the dealer that you buy or lease your car from. No one else!

5- What to Let the Salesperson Know

➤ Your first name.

➤ The make, model and trim level you're interested in seeing.

➤ Color is optional and nothing more is needed.

6- Auditioning a Prospective New Car

The following are considerations to be made when viewing a car:

✧ Walk around the car to see if you like its size and style.

✧ Bring a tape measure to see if the car will fit in your garage.
✧ Open all the doors for viewing the interior.
✧ Loading and unloading should be easy on your back.
✧ Make sure there is ample storage space.
✧ Consider ease of entry and exit.
✧ Check for availability of power outlets.
✧ Check to see how well the seats fold down and recline.

7- Before the Test Drive

For the sake of safety, it's a good idea to acquaint yourself with the following interior features so you won't have your attention drawn away during the test drive:

✧ Moonroof
✧ Sun visors
✧ Windows
✧ Door locks
✧ Mirrors
✧ Turn signals
✧ Cruise control buttons
✧ Emergency flashers
✧ Emergency brake
✧ Windshield wipers
✧ Headlight switch
✧ Radio system
✧ Air conditioner and heater controls
✧ Storage compartments available from driver's seat

Ask your salesperson about any other power buttons or controls.

8- The Test Drive

Choose a route that will show the vehicle's performance and handling qualities. Keep the radio turned off during some portion of the test drive so you can listen to the car. Keep in mind that this is *your* test drive; focus on the car and don't let the salesperson distract you. While on the test drive, pay attention to:

✧ Ease of visibility
✧ Interior feel
✧ Ride quality
✧ Acceleration
✧ Sounds
✧ Blind spots
✧ Visibility of gauges
✧ Handling
✧ Braking
✧ Pedal position

- ✧ Turning radius
- ✧ Ease of access to all controls
- ✧ Smooth transmission shifts
- ✧ Driving position (seat and steering wheel)

- ✧ Air conditioner
- ✧ Heater

9- Nighttime Lighting Test

In a darkened area, check if the instrument panel lights and interior lights are to your liking. You may need to drive the car at night to test the headlights and fog lights.

Some salespeople can be very pleasant and take great care of their customer. If you have built a relationship with your sales person, the desire to keep working with them can be very strong. After all, good help is hard to find. But keep in mind that getting the best price from a salesperson is usually a very challenging ordeal and you may end up with the feeling that it wasn't the best deal after all... and it usually isn't.

☞ If getting the absolute lowest price possible is your top priority, get off the lot and follow the guidelines in Chapter 11, "Locate and Negotiate by Phone."

5

Your Trade-In's Value

In This Chapter

The following websites will help you determine your car's retail (street) value and what a dealer will pay you for it. With this information you will know whether to sell your car on your own or trade it in to the dealer.

♦ Always negotiate the price of your new car before negotiating the price of your trade-in. These are two separate issues. Never even mention trade-in until after you finalize negotiations on your new car. If a dealer asks if you have a trade-in, simply say no for now.

1- Pricing Sources

In order to get the most money for your used car, you need to know the year, make, model, mileage, options and condition.

1. Go to the following websites to view used car book values:

www.edmunds.com
Click on **TMV** (True Market Value)

www.kbb.com
On home page, click on **Trade-In Value** or **Private Party Value**

♦ "Book" trade-in value is usually higher than what a dealer will actually pay.

2. The following websites contain automobile classified listings locally and nationally for price comparisons. Look at cars similar to yours and you'll get a good idea of the current asking prices. These prices are usually negotiable. Dealer prices are typically higher than private party ads.

www.autotrader.com

www.cars.com

3. Check the local newspaper classified ads and local auto trader magazines for similar vehicles. Call some ads to help you determine your car's value.

4. For those of you who don't have access to the Internet, call your bank or library reference desk and ask for the *Kelley Blue Book* high and low prices. They have the same editions as car dealerships.

♦ Calling a dealership for a book value may not be the best way to go. They may quote you a lower price than it's true value in hopes of buying your car cheap.

2- Dealing With The Dealer

If you decide to trade in your vehicle to a dealership, your used vehicle pricing information from above will help you negotiate a higher trade-in value. If a dealership offers a high value for your trade-in, it's generally because they are making a large profit on your new vehicle purchase. Make sure you negotiated well on your new car.

Selling your vehicle on your own usually brings more money than trading it in to a dealer.

3- Leased Cars

Call your leasing company and ask them what the buy-out is on your leased car. That's the amount you would pay to purchase the car from your lease company that day. Look up the book values and the classified listings at the websites listed above and you'll have a good idea where you stand financially on the car.

♦ Most people owe more on their car than it's current trade-in or retail value. This overage can be rolled into the monthly payments on a new car purchase or lease which will make the payments higher.

4- End-of-Lease Term Options

➤ Return the vehicle to the dealer.

➤ Sell the vehicle privately, pay off the debt and keep the profit (if any).

6

Dealers' Hidden Profits

In This Chapter

Knowing about the dealer's hidden profits gives you the edge necessary to getting the absolute lowest price possible. If you apply the dealer's hidden money wisely into the negotiations, you will not experience any buyer's remorse after the deal is completed. The key to uncovering this information is knowing where to find it and how to ask for it.

1- Manufacturer-to-Dealer Incentives: National, Regional and Quota Based

Manufacturers create various dealer incentive programs to provide the dealer a reason to move a specific model and an opportunity to increase their profit margin.

♦ Dealerships prefer the salespeople and consumer not know about manufacturer-to-dealer incentives. You should lower the negotiated price of the car by all or most of this incentive.

Typical reasons for manufacturer-to-dealer incentives:

- ➤ A new model is coming out and the manufacturer wants to sell the old models

- ➤ A specific model is selling slowly

- ➤ It's a slow time of the year

- ➤ The manufacturer is pushing for a rapid increase in sales

- ➤ The manufacturer is responding to its competition

2- National Dealer Incentives

A National Dealer Incentive is money given by the manufacturer to their dealers nationwide.

To determine if there is a national dealer incentive on a specific new car, refer to the independent websites below. These websites are updated sporadically. Therefore, it's best that you go to every site to compile the most accurate information.

www.autobytel.com   4★
Click on **Research**

www.autopedia.com   4★
Scroll and click on **Consumer incentives and rebates**

www.autosite.com   5★
Click on **Research**

www.edmunds.com   5★
Click on **Incentives and Rebates**

www.intellichoice.com   4.5★
Scroll and click on **Rebates and Incentives**

www.kbb.com   5★

The following guidelines will help you to verify the information you find on the Internet.

☞ If you prefer to by-pass this next section, go to Chapter 11, "Locate and Negotiate by Phone." Various tips on how to get the absolute lowest price possible are included.

3- Verifying the Current Dealer Incentive

Use the following system to verify your website findings or to determine the actual dealer incentive amount.

Call a dealership and ask to speak with the fleet manager. If the dealership does not have a fleet manager, ask for the sales manager. The manager is the correct person (not a salesperson) that will know if a dealer incentive exists on a particular car and its amount.

You must verify a dealer incentive amount with two or three dealerships before you can be certain you have the accurate dealer incentive. To do this, call the fleet manager and ask the following question verbatim.

Dealer Incentive Question: *"I'm getting ready to buy a new* (your chosen make and model) *and I would like to know if there is a* (example: $2,000) *manufacturer-to-dealer incentive on this vehicle right now. Is this amount accurate?"*

For the purposes of this example, the websites showed $1,000 dealer incentive so you should start by doubling it to $2,000. Doing this will enable you to get accurate information more quickly.

Possible answers:

A- If the fleet manager says "No" to your $2,000 amount, then ask: *"How much is it?"* If they say it's $1,000, you have verified your website research. To be certain you have the accurate dealer incentive amount, you might want to call another dealership and repeat the **Dealer Incentive Question.**

B- If the fleet manager says: "No, (to $2,000) it's $1,500," you have established a new possible dealer incentive amount. Call another dealership and repeat the **Dealer Incentive Question.**

C- If the fleet manager says: "Yes" (to $2,000) you have either guessed correctly or there is actually a larger dealer incentive available.

Don't let the first yes convince you. Call a different dealership and repeat the **Dealer Incentive Question,** but raise the $2,000 figure to $3,000 in order to establish a new possible amount.

Repeat these steps until you get at least two or three dealerships that agree on the same amount. This will be your verified national manufacturer-to-dealer incentive and will help you reduce the price of your new car.

4- Regional Dealer Incentives

A Regional Dealer Incentive is money given by the manufacturer to the dealers in a specific region of the country. If the manufacturer is offering a Regional Dealer Incentive, they typically will not offer a National Incentive at the same time.

Dealerships are not inclined to disclose regional dealer incentives. Information on the amount of this regional incentive is one more source that will help reduce the price of the car.

> ♦ Limited production or in-demand cars are either a brand new model or a major freshening up of an existing model. These cars are fed slowly into the marketplace and therefore, the manufacturer does not offer the dealer any incentive.

To find out if a regional dealer incentive exists, go to www.edmunds.com (click on: **Regional incentives**). If you discover a regional dealer incentive for your area, ask the dealer the following question: *"I understand there is a* (example: $2,000) *regional dealer incentive on a* (your chosen make and model) *right now. Is this incentive amount accurate?"*

5- Quota-Based Sales Incentives

A Quota-Based Sales Incentive is money given by the manufacturer to the dealers based on a specified number of cars sold by the end-of-quarter (March, June, September, December) or end-of-month. You're more likely to receive a better price at the end-of-quarter than end-of-month.

The following is an sample to show how the program might work:

For example, the first quota level, the manufacturer may pay the dealer $50 per car for the first 10 sold, equaling $500. Not until the 10th car is sold will the dealer get the $500. If the dealer sells nine cars or less, they do not receive any of this sales incentive money.

For the second quota level, the manufacturer may pay the dealer $100 per car if they sell a minimum of 50. Not until the 50th car is sold will this $100 per car incentive apply. If they sell 49 cars, they get $50 each, which equals $2,450. But if they sell the 50th car, they will receive a total of $5,000 which is $2,550 more profit above the 49 car total.

For the third quota level, the manufacturer may pay the dealer $200 per car if they sell a minimum of 100. Not until the 100th car is sold will this $200 per car incentive apply. If they sell 99 cars, they get $100 each, which equals $9,900. But if they sell the 100th car, they will receive a total of $20,000 which is $10,100 more profit above the 99 car total.

A dealership that needs just one more sale to meet their next quota level will sell at a price that is substantially below all other dealerships. If they're looking at making a $20,000 profit in incentive money from a car sale, it's in their best interest to reduce the price by thousands of dollars. In these situations, both the dealership and the consumer profit tremendously. This is the kind of deal where a little effort on the part of the consumer may have a surprisingly large pay off.

♦ **A dealership usually does not reveal their sales quota status. You only find out if they accept your low offer.**

Here is a question you can ask your dealership contact person: *"I don't know if there's any profit for you in my offer, but I've heard of special incentives that the manufacturer gives the dealer once in a while. Can you sell me the car for $1,000* (or more) *below dealer's invoice?"* If this is a ridiculous offer, asking the question this way will keep the dealer from hanging up on you. If they say "no", ask them, *"How close to that offer can you sell it for?"* They will usually give you their rock bottom price.

To determine which dealership is about to meet their next quota level:

- ➤ Make your offer within the last two days of the month / quarter
- ➤ Make a very low offer and see if they accept it
- ➤ Keep calling dealerships within your travel limits until you find that hungry dealer that will accept your offer

6- The Holdback Money

This is money paid to dealers by most manufacturers for each car sold typically based on one to three percent of the Manufacturer's Suggested Retail Price. The dealer is very unlikely to give up this money; but knowing that it exists will put you in a better negotiating position.

☞ To determine if a holdback exists, go to www.edmunds.com and click on **Advice**.

7- Not-So-Hidden Dealer Profits

Apart from the manufacturer-to-dealer incentive programs, there are other sources by which the dealer may increase their profits.

These are:

- ➤ Extended warranty
- ➤ Maintenance package
- ➤ Insurance
- ➤ Dealer installed accessories or car treatments
- ➤ Trade-in
- ➤ High interest rates (leasing and financing)

- ♦ Leasing provides the dealer with more profit than financing while a cash purchase provides the thinnest profit margin.

7

Manufacturers' Warranties

In This Chapter
1- Bumper to Bumper
2- Drive Train
3- Rust/Corrosion
4- Roadside Assistance
5- If it's a Lemon

The factory warranty is a promise by the manufacturer to repair any defective part covered by the warranty while it is in effect. This is an area that many people pay little attention to. It should be looked at closely because it can add considerable value to a car. Both the length of the factory warranty and the length of free scheduled maintenance (if any) should be looked at closely. This segment will show you what factory warranties are all about.

Manufacturer Warranty repair work is done at all franchised dealerships nationwide, not only the dealership you purchased your car from. The manufacturer pays for warranty repairs performed at a franchised dealership but not at an independent auto repair shop.

To keep the manufacturer's warranty in effect, you must follow the manufacturer's scheduled maintenance requirements found in the owners manual. Licensed independent repair shops can do these scheduled maintenance services but are not authorized to perform manufacturer's warranty repair work.

Regardless of who performs the scheduled maintenance services, it's best to keep all your receipts to show what work was done for your car's warranty protection.

1- Bumper to Bumper

The basic factory warranty is bumper to bumper except for some wear items such as tires and brake pads. The battery may be warranted for about one year or twelve thousand miles. Some higher-end manufacturers include free scheduled maintenance on the entire car with their basic factory warranty. All you need to purchase are tires and maybe brake pads. Consider the high cost of scheduled maintenance when making your buying decision.

2- Drive Train

The drive train includes all internal parts for the engine, transmission, front wheel drive, rear wheel drive and all wheel drive systems. Some manufacturers extend the drive train warranty beyond the bumper-to-bumper warranty.

3- Rust/Corrosion

Surface rust on a painted surface may be covered for one year, while rust-through on body panels can be up to five years. Rust-through corrosion on the chassis and body undercarriage may be included for the full term of the warranty. Reading the warranty details closely will give you all the information you need.

4- Roadside Assistance

This helps if you:

> Lock yourself out of your car

> Run out of gas

➤ Get a flat tire

➤ Break down and need a tow

Some manufacturers offer a loaner car if you break down fifty miles or more from your home. They will also return your car once it's been repaired.

If a manufacturer does not offer "roadside assistance," they will usually pay for the cost of towing to the nearest dealership if the breakdown is covered under the factory warranty.

Smog emission components are covered beyond the bumper-to-bumper warranty.

Different models built by the same manufacturer may vary in warranty coverage and free scheduled maintenance. Call the dealer and ask if there is more or less factory warranty coverage on the model you are interested in than on the other models in the manufacturer's line up. Also, ask if the manufacturer is currently offering free scheduled maintenance on the specific model you are interested in.

For current factory warranty specifications, go to www.cars.com. Click on Manufacturer **Warranty Comparison**. If you have further questions, call the Manufacturer's Consumer Hotline Number located in the Appendix.

5- If It's a Lemon

A vehicle is considered a lemon when it has a reoccurring problem while still under factory warranty. If the problem persists after several attempts to repair the vehicle, some states require the manufacturer to buy the vehicle back from you. You'll be charged for the mileage up to the first documented repair attempt. The sooner you document the problem with the dealership, the more the manufacturer reimburses you.

☞ See Manufacturer's Warranty Chart in the Appendix for an at-a-glance view.

8

The Extended Warranty

In This Chapter

1 - Pros and Cons
2 - What to Ask
3 - Of Interest

Should I buy an extended warranty? This is a typical question that many new car buyers face and not knowing the answer can cost them hundreds or thousands of dollars. There are numerous things to consider in order to make an informed decision. Don't just plop down a pile of your cash. Read on.

An extended warranty is an insurance policy that extends beyond the factory warranty and can be similar to your factory warranty. Either the manufacturer or a third party company can offer it.

To determine whether you want an extended warranty, call the dealership's service department and ask about the reliability of the car of interest for the specified time and mileage you want (example: 6 years/ 75,000 miles). They are not sales people and will usually give you an unbiased response.

1- Pros and Cons

Why you might want to buy one:

> ➤ An extended warranty that covers the length of time between the end of the factory warranty and up to 100,000 miles could save you money on expensive repairs.

> ➤ When you sell your car the resale value will be higher if an extended warranty is active, putting the private party buyer's mind at ease.

Extended warranties are transferable only to private party buyers, not a dealer. If a dealer buys your car, the extended warranty is permanently voided and cannot be passed on to the next buyer.

If never used, some extended warranties can be sold back to the issuing company for a full or partial refund before or at expiration. Ask.

Why you may not want to buy one:

> ➤ You typically sell your car before the factory warranty expires.

> ➤ You will return your leased car before the factory warranty expires.

> ➤ The car you are buying is known to be reliable for the period you intend to own it. In that case, the cost of the extended warranty will outweigh the cost of expected repairs (example: Lexus, Toyota, Acura, Honda).

Recall information at the following websites can give you an idea of how well a vehicle is built:

www.alldata.com   5★
Click on **Recalls and Technical Service Bulletins Titles**

www.autoweb.com   4★
Click on **Research New Vehicles** then click on **Recalls**

National Highway Traffic Safety Administration
www.nhtsa.dot.gov   5★
Click on **Recalls**. View one, two and three-year histories of reported problems

www.consumerreports.org   5★
This fee-based website offers the reliability of an existing model

2- What to Ask

You can obtain information on the manufacturer's extended warranty from the dealership's finance manager. Ask for the name of their top-of-the-line extended warranty on the vehicle you've chosen. Make sure to ask if it is being offered by the manufacturer or a third party extended warranty company. You also need to know the deductible (usually $50 or $100) and the retail price. Experience has shown that a zero dollar deductible is a great way to go and doesn't cost much more. Ask for the duration of the extended warranty. (This will usually be six or seven years and between 70,000 to 100,000 miles.)

Extended warranties can also be purchased online at the following websites. You should compare the dealership's extended warranty closely (item for item) to any offered on the Internet:

www.1sourceautowarranty.com
View prices and contract instantly

www.carsdirect.com
Click on **Extended Warranties**

www.certifiedcarcare.com
User friendly site. Click on **Instant Quote Click Here**

www.warrantydirect.com

www.warrantygold.com

When an extended warranty is not backed by the manufacturer, the following questions should be asked (to any third party extended warranty company) even if it's being offered through a dealership:

1. Does it include a deductible? ($50, $100, etc.)

2. Is there an additional deductible required for further problems during the same repair visit? ($0 deductible is best)

3. Are repairs allowed at an independent mechanic other than the dealership?

4. Is an independent mechanic required to call the warranty company for repair authorization? If so, how long before repairs are authorized?

5. Are repairs authorized nationwide?

6. Does the warranty company pay the mechanic directly or are you required to pay first. If so, how long will it take to get reimbursed?

7. Does the warranty specify new factory parts or are used and reconditioned parts allowed also?

8. Can you transfer the warranty upon the sale of your car and if so, how much is the transfer fee?

9. Are the following services included: auto rental, motel, towing and roadside assistance?

3- Of Interest

Dealers offer both manufacturer extended warranties and independent extended warranties.

To insure that the extended warranty company pays for repairs, have all factory-scheduled maintenance performed and keep the records.

If you would like to cancel your extended warranty for any reason, you generally have 30 days from the date of purchase for a full refund or credit toward your loan.

Buying an extended warranty elsewhere will be a separate purchase. You may choose to include the cost of an extended warranty into the car's financing, therefore purchasing it from the dealer.

You do not need to purchase an extended warranty the day you buy a new car. Some extended warranty companies will sell you the same extended warranty at a similar price as long as you buy it shortly before your factory warranty expires. Buying it from a dealer later will usually cost you more.

Sometimes a dealership will claim that in order to be approved for a loan you must purchase an extended warranty. A loan approval is based on your credit rating only and therefore, you do not need to purchase an extended warranty.

If you are pre-approved by a bank or credit union for a car loan, they will usually be willing to increase your loan amount to cover an extended warranty even on a maximized loan.

Before you finalize negotiations on your car, you should decide if you want an extended warranty through the dealership. This is the best time to get the lowest price on an extended warranty from a dealer.

☞   See Chapter 11, #15 "Negotiating the Extended Warranty."

9

Auto Leasing Simplified

In This Chapter

Leasing is the most confusing area to consumers when considering a new car. There are so many variables it can be overwhelming. Deciding whether to finance or lease is completely explained here to make things easy for you.

1- About Lease Advertisements

Television and newspaper ads that use attention getting low monthly lease payments can get your adrenaline levels way up. Wow! You can get a really cool car for a monthly payment that you'll have no problem dealing with. But once you read the fine print, a very different story emerges.

First of all, mileage limits may be too low for your needs, with an extra per mile charge above the lease term limits. At a typical penalty rate of fifteen to thirty cents per mile, you will be charged an extra $150 to $300 for every 1,000 miles you drive over your limits.

An advertised zero down at contract signing on a lease might not really mean zero down. The dealer will typically include a few fees. Security deposit and other fees can raise the amount due at lease signing into the thousands of dollars.

Also, the monthly payments on these lease deals may be required for as long as 48 to 60 months rather than a more typical 24 or 36 month lease. A dealership can squeeze much more profit out of a 48 to 60 month lease than a shorter lease.

2- Finance vs. Lease

If your concern is which offers a better tax advantage, financing or leasing, a good accountant is the best person to guide you in this decision.

Typical leases are 24 to 36 months. The amount-due-at-lease-signing and monthly lease payments are typically lower than a down payment with monthly finance payments on a loan.

For the purpose of getting lower lease payments, some people will lease beyond the manufacturer's warranty (such as 48 to 60 months). It is preferable to lease for the length (or shorter) of the manufacturer's warranty (see Appendix for "Manufacturer's Warranty Chart") so you don't encounter repair bills. Buying an extended warranty to cover the extra lease time beyond the factory warranty will increase your monthly lease payment closer to a finance payment. This does not make good financial sense.

3- Typical Buyer Traits

- ✧ High mileage driver
- ✧ Takes pride in ownership
- ✧ Keeps vehicle for many years
- ✧ Carries passengers
- ✧ Doesn't mind selling a car
- ✧ Likes to customize
- ✧ Lots of wear and use
- ✧ Drives rough roads
- ✧ Hauls dogs and cargo
- ✧ Frugal with their money

4- Typical Lessee Traits

- ✧ Needs the tax advantage
- ✧ Drives mainly for business
- ✧ Has minimal down payment
- ✧ Wants a pricier car
- ✧ Having a car worth cash isn't important
- ✧ Low mileage driver
- ✧ Likes to drive new cars
- ✧ Doesn't like to sell a car
- ✧ Can't afford to buy a car

Bold terms defined on page 58

Sample Comparison Chart

5- Finance   vs.   Lease

Based on 15,000 miles driven per year

Window sticker price	$25,000	Window sticker price	$25,000
Negotiated final price	$23,000	Negotiated final price	$23,000
Down payment	$4,000	**Amount-due-at-lease-signing**	$1,200
Amt. financed (fees incl.)	**$21,280**	Price of car plus bank fee	$23,500
Loan term (# of months)	36	**Lease term** (# of months)	36
End-of-loan **trade-in value**	$13,000	End-of-lease trade-in value	$13,000
Monthly loan payment	$590	**Monthly lease payment**	$332
A) Total of all payments	$25,240	A) Total of all payments	$13,152
B) Sell now or keep paying	$13,000	B) **End-of-lease fees**	$500 (+ / -)
C) Your cost to now (A-B)	**$12,240**	C) Your cost to now (A+B)	**$13,652**
			(Car turned-in to dealer)

Comparison Chart

6- Finance   vs.   Lease

Based on ____,000 miles driven per year

Window sticker price	_____	Window sticker price	_____
Negotiated final price	_____	Negotiated final price	_____
Down payment	_____	**Amount-due-at-lease-signing**	_____
Amount financed	_____	Price of car plus bank fee	_____
Loan term (# of months)	_____	**Lease term** (# of months)	_____
End-of-loan trade-in value	_____	End-of-lease trade-in value	_____
Monthly loan payment	_____	**Monthly lease payment**	_____
A) Total of all payments	_____	A) Total of all payments	_____
B) End-of-loan trade-in value	_____	B) **End-of-lease fees**	_____
C) Your cost to now (A–B)	_____	C) Your cost to now (A+B)	_____

(Car turned-in to dealer)

7- Leasing Tips

Bold terms defined on page 58

1. If the model you like comes equipped differently from one vehicle to the next, the **window sticker price** will vary. Therefore, you should negotiate from the **dealer's invoice** price (what a dealer pays for a car).

Vehicles that are equipped similarly from one to the next are also priced the same. In this case, it's better to negotiate the **monthly lease payment** and **total-due-at-lease-signing** than to negotiate from the dealer's invoice price. This establishes the lowest possible window sticker price automatically and eliminates all possibility of dealer hidden fees.

☞ For more on negotiating a lease, see Chapter 11, #17 "Getting the First Lease Quote from a Dealer."

2. Aim for a low **drive-off** (same as total-due-at-lease-signing) amount. Leases are structured based on two financial variables, the **monthly lease payment** and the **drive-off** amount. The drive-off amount is a culmination of several fees. If you choose to lower your drive-off amount, some or all of the drive-off fees will be included into the monthly lease payment.

3. The first few weeks of a new model's introduction (could be any month of the year) is when you will get the lowest lease payments. However, at times the manufacturer will offer a lease special later in the year when lease payments would be typically higher.

4. Registration renewal is generally due every year (12, 24, 36 and 48 months). A 30 month (two and a half year), 39month (three and a quarter year) or 42 month (three and a half year) lease has you pay for something you won't have. You will pay a full year's registration fee but only have the vehicle a few months before having to turn it in.

5. If you worry about money spent to bring your leased vehicle back to acceptable condition (new tires, tune-up, body work) before turning it in, then consider the "peace of mind" of ownership.

6. Most leases require more insurance coverage with lower deductibles, thereby raising your insurance costs.

7. If you would like to save interest by paying all your lease payments up front, ask the finance manager how this works.

8. Some people plan to buy the car at the end of a lease. For them, a lower **residual value** (the value of the car at the end of the lease) is preferable. Although this raises the monthly lease payment, it allows them to finance less money when it comes time to purchase.

9. Paying for additional miles up front in your monthly lease payment rather than at the end of the lease will cost you substantially less money. The unused prepaid mileage may be refundable but ask before you sign the contract.

10. Some leases do not allow travel into Mexico or Canada. Ask the dealer or read the contract.

8- Before Turning In Your Leased Vehicle

➤ Find a dealer to inspect your car free of charge a few weeks before you turn it in so you know what to repair. If you get the repairs done on your own, it will cost you less than what the leasing company will charge you. Be aware that you could be penalized for lesser quality repair work.

➤ If the dealer assesses **wear and usage** too high, turn the car in to another dealer (same manufacturer).

9- Lease-End

When you enter into a lease, you are agreeing to follow the factory-scheduled maintenance on your vehicle. You should keep all the receipts to prove that your vehicle was maintained or you could be penalized. At the end of the lease, expect your vehicle to undergo a **wear and use** inspection. You are liable for any extraordinary wear on the vehicle. The key concerns are dents, dings, scratches, upholstery stains and tears, missing pieces, cracked or broken light lenses and glass, worn tires and excessive mileage. If the vehicle appears to have been well cared for, an inspector may overlook some of the minor damage.

♦ Before you lease, you may be able to get the dealer to sign an
agreement to the effect that you won't have to pay for certain
types of wear and usage. This is not standard policy, but can
be a point of negotiation.

10- End-of-Term Options

➤ Return the vehicle to the dealer.

➤ Buy the vehicle for the **residual value**. Some leasing companies
have low interest rate financing available when your lease ends.

➤ Lease another vehicle upon returning your currently leased
vehicle.

➤ Sell the vehicle, pay off the residual value and keep the profit (if
any).

➤ Extend the lease typically 1 to 6 months, usually at the same
monthly lease payment.

➤ Re-lease the vehicle with a new contract for 24 to 36 months
(not available with all lease companies).

11- Verify Your Own Lease

The following lease verification formula will verify your **monthly lease
payment** and **drive-off** (total-due-at-lease-signing) amount only after you
have finalized negotiations with the dealer. If the dealer mis-calculated or
included hidden fees, with this formula, they will all be revealed.

The dealer may say you cannot calculate a lease on paper. Be assured,
with the following verification formula you can. By using this formula, you
will save the amount of money it would cost for a computer leasing
program.

Step 1: You and the dealer must agree upon your monthly lease
payment (tax included) and the drive-off amount *before* you can use the
following lease verification formula. All negotiations must be finalized.

Step 2: Call your dealership contact person and ask for the amounts that have the letter "D" (for Dealer) beside them in the formula and write the amount on the line.

◆ **The acquisition (bank) fee is included in the monthly lease payment or the drive-off. Not both. Ask your contact person which one it is.**

Step 3: Proceed with your calculator to complete the rest of the formula. Fill in every line with either an amount or a zero (exception: line 16 is a lease term).

A completed Sample Lease Verification Formula has been included for your reference.

Step 4: If a calculation doesn't add-up properly, call your contact person and ask them to explain the error.

12- Sample Lease Verification Formula

For **Monthly Lease Payment**

Bold terms defined on page 58

Final negotiated amounts recorded:

Monthly lease payment   **$289.69** (tax included)

Total-due-at-lease-signing   **$2255.94** (Drive-Off)

Lease term: miles per year = **12,000**   # of months = **36**

1. Vehicle price $22,500
2. **Bank (Acquisition) fee** $400
3. **Capitalized cost** (1 + 2) $22,900
4. Debt on your trade-in .... none
5. Add-on (example: alarm) .... none
6. Other fees (if any) .... none
7. **Gross cap cost** (add 3 thru 6) $22,900
8. **Cash to reduce payments** $1,000
   (Different from **Total-Due-At-Lease-Signing**)
9. **Trade-in allowance** .... none
10. **Rebate / Incentive** $500
11. Other discount .... none
12. **Cap cost reduction** (add 8 thru 11) $1,500
13. **Adjusted cap cost** (7 - 12) $21,400
14. **Residual**   (cars end-of-lease value) $17,050
15. **Depreciation** (13 - 14) $4,350
16. **Lease term** (# of months) 36
17. Average monthly depreciation (15 divided by 16) $120.83
18. Money factor (leasings version of % rate) .... .00385
19. Average monthly **rent charge** (13 + 14 x 18) $148.03
20. **Base monthly payment** (17 + 19) $268.86
21. Tax on monthly payment (20 x 7.75% sales tax) $20.83

TOTAL MONTHLY PAYMENT (20 + 21) **$289.69**

Sample Lease Verification Formula ...continued

For **Total-Due-At-Lease-Signing**

22. Bank fee .... none
23. **Security deposit** $400
24. State fees (license, tire, doc, etc.) $450
25. Cap reduction tax (#12 x sales tax) $116.25
26. Cash to reduce payment (same as #8) $1000
27. First monthly payment (same as #20) $268.86
28. Tax on first monthly payment (same as #21) $20.83

TOTAL-DUE-AT-LEASE-SIGNING (add 22 thru 28) **$2,255.94**

End-of-Lease Fees:

Disposal fee.. $300
Excess mileage .... .20
Purchase option fee .... none
Other fee .... none

13- Foolproof Lease Verification Formula
For Your **Monthly Lease Payment**
Bold terms defined on page 58

Record your final negotiated amounts:
Monthly lease payment $_____ (tax included)
Total-due-at-lease-signing $_____ **(Drive-Off)**
Lease term: miles per year = _____   # of months = _____

"**D**" = Ask **D**ealer
D 1. Vehicle price (final) .... 1_____
D 2. **Acquisition fee** .... 2_____
     (if included on line #2, line #22 must be $0)
   3. **Capitalized cost** (1 + 2) .... 3_____
   4. Debt on your **trade-in** .... 4_____
   5. Add-ons (example: alarm, CD) .... 5_____
   6. Other fees (if any) .... 6_____
     (If $0 **Drive-Off**, those fees go on line 6)
   7. **Gross capitalized cost** (add 3 thru 6) .... 7_____
D 8. **Cash to reduce payments** .... 8_____
     (#8 is different from **Total-Due-At-Lease-Signing**)
   9. **Trade-in allowance** .... 9_____
D 10. **Rebate / Incentive** .... 10_____
  11. Other discount .... 11_____
  12. **Cap cost reduction** (add 8 thru 11) .... 12_____
  13. **Adjusted cap cost** (7 - 12) .... 13_____
D 14. **Residual value** ($ amount, not a %) .... 14_____
  15. **Depreciation** (13 - 14) .... 15_____
  16. **Lease term** (# of months) .... 16_____
  17. Monthly depreciation (15 divided by 16)......... 17_____
D 18. **Money factor** .... 18_____
  19. Monthly **rent charge** (13 + 14 x 18) .... 19_____
  20. **Base monthly payment** (17 + 19) .... 20_____
  21. Tax on monthly payment (20 x your sales tax) .... 21_____

   TOTAL MONTHLY PAYMENT (20 + 21) .... $_____
                        (+ or - $1 from dealers quote)

Foolproof Lease Verification Formula ...continued

For Your **Total-Due-At-Lease-Signing**

D 22. Acquisition fee .... 22_____
     (if included on line #22, line #2 must be $0)
D 23. **Security deposit** .... 23_____
D 24. State fees (license, tire, doc, etc.) .... 24_____
     (get each amount and total them for line 24)
25. Cap cost reduction tax (#12 x your sales tax) .... 25_____
26. Cash to reduce payments (same as #8) .... 26_____
27. First monthly payment (same as #20) .... 27_____
28. Tax on first monthly payment (same as #21) .... 28_____

   TOTAL-DUE-AT-LEASE-SIGNING (add 22 thru 28) $_____
                              (+ or - $1 from dealers quote)

End-of-Lease Fees:

D 29. **Disposal fee** (may be negotiable) .... 29_____
D 30. **Excess mileage** .... 30_____
D 31. **Purchase option fee** .... 31_____
D 32. Other fee (if any) .... 32_____

Remember to ask: "Is it a **closed-end** or **open-end lease**?"
"Is **gap insurance** included?"

14- Money Factor Formula

The money factor on a lease is equivalent to the interest rate you pay on a loan. It's leasing terminology for interest rate. It's the interest you pay on your lease.

Dealerships may state the money factor in a variety of ways. For example: .00385, 3.85 or 385 with the last being the most common.

To calculate the interest rate equivalent of a money factor, follow one of the sample formulas below:

- ➤ 385 (money factor) x .024 = 9.24% (interest rate).

- ➤ 3.85 (money factor) x 2.4 = 9.24% (interest rate).

- ➤ .00385 (money factor) x 2400 = 9.24% (interest rate).

- ➤ 9.24% (interest rate) divided by 2400 = .00385 (money factor).

- ➤ .0924% (interest rate) divided by 24 = .00385 (money factor).

15- Money Factor Quick Reference Chart

042 = 1%	251 = 6%	459 = 11%
062 = 1.5%	271 = 6.5%	480 = 11.5%
083 = 2%	292 = 7%	501 = 12%
105 = 2.5%	313 = 7.5%	521 = 12.5%
125 = 3%	334 = 8%	542 = 13%
146 = 3.5%	355 = 8.5%	563 = 13.5%
167 = 4%	375 = 9%	584 = 14%
188 = 4.5%	396 = 9.5%	605 = 14.5%
209 = 5%	417 = 10%	626 = 15%
230 = 5.5%	438 = 10.5%	646 = 15.5%

16- Ballpark Monthly Lease Payment Chart

The monthly payments below are with zero down.
Discounts and cash down would lower these payments.
The **money factor** and **residual value** fluctuate the payment.
On a Lease Special, the monthly payments will be lower.

For a more expensive car than the chart shows, add the price of two cars
together to arrive at a monthly payment. (Remember, these are ballpark
figures only. Typical monthly lease payments tend to be lower).
Example: On a 36 month lease, a $50,000 car (see chart: $30,000 @ $560
a month plus $20,000 @ $380 a month) will equal a monthly payment of
$940.

Price of Vehicle	Lease Term (months)		
	24	36	48
$10,000	$220	$190	$170
$12,000	$260	$220	$200
$14,000	$300	$260	$240
$16,000	$340	$300	$270
$18,000	$380	$340	$310
$20,000	$420	**$380**	$350
$22,000	$460	$410	$370
$24,000	$500	$450	$410
$26,000	$540	$490	$450
$28,000	$580	$520	$480
$30,000	$620	**$560**	$510

For a lease quote on a specific car, go to www.carsdirect.com
Select a **Make** and **Model** then click **Go**.

17- Leasing Glossary

Bold terms in the chapter are defined here, in the glossary. The definitions are attached to terms most frequently used by dealers. If further help is needed to understand a term, call the finance manager at a dealership of your choice.

Acquisition Fee:
Also known as **assignment fee**, **bank fee**, **inception fee** or **initiation fee.** An up-front lender fee for processing and handling the lease. It is typically rolled into the monthly payments, but can be included in the **drive-off** amount. The fee typically ranges from $300-$800 and is set by the lender. It's non-refundable and is not included in all leases. It can be negotiated.

Adjusted Capitalized (cap) Cost:
Also known as **net capitalized cost.** The amount of money arrived at after the **capitalized cost reduction** has been subtracted from the **gross capitalized cost**. A key component when calculating monthly lease payments.

Amount-Due-At-Lease-Signing: See **drive-off.**

Assignment Fee: See **acquisition fee.**

Bank Fee: See **acquisition fee.**

Base Interest Rate: See **rent charge.**

Base Monthly Payment:
This is your monthly payment minus the sales tax.

Buy Fee: See **purchase option fee.**

Buyout:
If you want to purchase your leased vehicle at any time during your lease, the amount the lender quotes is the price you must pay.

Capitalized (cap) Cost:
The final negotiated price of the vehicle plus the **acquisition fee** (if any).

Capitalized (cap) Cost Reduction:
Includes the total of the following items (if any): Cash down payment,

vehicle **trade-in allowance, rebate, incentive** or any **discount** that lowers the price of the new car ultimately lowering the monthly payment.

Cash down payment:
Additional money you pay up front to lower your monthly lease payments.

Cash to Reduce Payments: See **cash down payment.**

Closed-end Lease:
This is a type of lease you walk away from at lease-end with no further financial obligation, except for **excess wear and use**, mileage and **disposition fee** (if any). The other option is an **open-end lease.**

Default Penalties:
Penalties you are required to pay if you do not pay your lease payments. You could lose your **security deposit**, have to pay remaining obligations with the lease, pay legal fees and costs to repossess the vehicle.

Dealer Discount:
Any amount the dealer reduces from the **window sticker price** voluntarily.

Dealer Prep:
A fee charged by the dealer to get a new car ready to sell.

Dealer's Invoice:
The amount the dealer pays the manufacturer for a vehicle. If there are any manufacturer-to-dealer incentives available, the dealer will pay less.

Depreciation:
The amount charged in the monthly lease payment for the vehicle's decline in value over the **term** of the **lease** for normal use. The depreciation amount charged varies among lenders. **Adjusted cap cost** minus the **residual** equals the **depreciation.**

Destination Charge:
The fee charged by the manufacturer to the dealer for shipping the vehicle to the dealership.

Discount:
Incentives, rebates or discounts given to the customer by the manufacturer or dealer. Taxes typically need to be paid on discounts.

Disposal Fee:
Also known as **disposition fee** or **termination fee**. A fee (in your contract) charged by most lenders at lease end to cover the costs for transporting, detailing and selling the car (usually at auction). The lender usually sets the fee (if any) between $250 and $400. You may not be charged this fee if you lease another same make vehicle. A **security deposit** can also be applied towards the disposal fee. May be negotiable.

Disposition Fee: See **disposal fee.**

Down Payment:
The amount you pay at the time you sign the contract when financing a vehicle purchase. This term is used incorrectly at times in a lease, when the proper term is **drive-off.**

Drive Off:
Also known as **amount-due-at-lease-signing** and **total-due-at-lease-signing**. In financing, it is called the **down payment**. This amount includes all or some of the following: vehicle **trade-in allowance, acquisition fee**, first **monthly payment**, refundable **security deposit**, first year's license fee, cash you pay to lower your monthly payments and sales tax on the **cap cost reduction.**
Zero drive-off means you drive-off without paying any money. If you want a zero drive-off, then your monthly payments will be higher. You need good credit for a zero drive-off.

Early Termination:
A clause in many lease contracts that allows you to end the lease early. You will have to include the amount you owe above the car's actual retail value into your new car loan or lease payments or sell the car and write a separate check to the lease company to cover the loss on the sale.

Early Termination Fee:
In some leases, a fee is charged if you turn in your vehicle before lease-end. Some lenders waive this fee at times.

End-Of-Lease Fees:
All the charges that might apply when you return the leased vehicle. Example: **Excess mileage, default penalties, excess wear and use** and **disposition fee**. You may be able to negotiate the final amount.

Excess Mileage:
You will pay an added fee on miles driven above the pre-agreed mileage allowance, typically from 10,000-15,0000 miles per year. Charges typically range from fifteen to thirty cents per mile.

Excess Wear and Use:
Also known as **wear and use, wear and usage.** The amount of wear a vehicle receives during its **lease term**. Subject to interpretation by the lender. Each leasing company will vary in their guidelines. Many lease-returnees are surprised by how "large" their bill is.

Final Costs: See **end-of-lease fees.**

Gap Insurance:
May be called gap protection. This insurance covers the difference between what your insurance pays and what your lease company demands when a vehicle is stolen or totaled.
Example: Your insurance company pays the lease company $20,000 for the leased vehicle. Your lease company values the vehicle at $25,000. Gap insurance covers the $5,000.
If you don't have gap insurance, the money will come out of your pocket. Make sure gap insurance is included in your loan or lease contract or get it from your insurance company at a substantial savings.

Gross Capitalized (cap) Cost:
This is the final price of the vehicle. It includes items such as: price of vehicle, **acquisition fee**, service agreement, insurance and any prior loan or lease balance.

Incentive:
Manufacturer's money given to the dealer to help sell (lease) a specific model. The dealer may pass some or all of this money onto the consumer.

Inception Fee: See **acquisition fee.**

Initiation Fee: See **acquisition fee.**

Lease:
A contracted agreement between a lender **(lessor)** and a customer **(lessee)** in which the customer pays for the usage of a vehicle owned by the lender over a specified period of time.

Lease Factor: See **money factor.**

Lease Fee: See **rent charge.**

Lease Term:
Also known as **term**. Length of lease. The number of months and miles of usage allowed in the contract.

Lessee:
You, the customer.

Lessor:
The dealer, auto maker, bank or independent leasing company that buys the vehicle from the dealer and then leases it to a customer (**lessee**).

Level Yield Factor: See **money factor.**

Manufacturer's Suggested Retail Price:
See **Monroney Sticker.** Also know as **MSRP** or **window sticker price**. The printed retail price on a sheet of paper pasted on the window of a new car. Also, the starting point from where negotiations usually begin with the dealer.
Note: On limited production or in-demand cars, an additional dealer mark-up will be pasted near the MSRP on the window. If you are searching for one of these cars, ask for the MSRP, *then* ask: "What is your window sticker price?" (dealer mark-up)

Mileage Allowance:
A lease includes a specific number of miles to be driven per year. Beyond that, you pay extra. Amount of miles differ from lease to lease (typically from 10,000 to 20,000 miles).

Money Factor:
Also known as **base interest rate, lease factor** or **level yield factor.** This is lease terminology equivalent to "interest rate" and is negotiable.

Use the following formulas to calculate the money factor, depending on how the dealer presents it to you:
1) 3.85 (money factor) x 2.4 = 9.24% interest rate.
2) 385 (money factor) x .024 = 9.24% interest rate.
3) .00385 (money factor) x 2400 = 9.24% interest rate.
4) 9.24% (interest rate) divided by 2400 = .00385 (money factor).

5) .0924 (interest rate) divided by 24 = .00385 (money factor).

Monroney Sticker:
Also know as the **window sticker.** A printed sheet of paper pasted on the window of a new car. Every new car legally must have one. It identifies the car by vehicle identification number (VIN), year, make, model, trim level, color, standard features, options, packages, includes the Manufacturer's Suggested Retail Price (MSRP) and several other details about that specific vehicle. It is more commonly known as the window sticker.

Monthly Lease Payment:
As with a loan, most customers pay for a lease on a monthly basis. The amount you write the check for.

MSRP: See **Monroney Sticker.**

Net Capitalized Cost: See **adjusted capitalized cost.**

Open-end Lease:
If the vehicle's actual value at the end of the lease term is less than the **residual value**, you the customer will pay the difference, usually a sizable balloon payment. Most leases are now closed-end which are safer.

Option To Buy: See **purchase option.**

Purchase Option:
The opportunity to purchase the vehicle before or at lease-end.

Purchase Option Fee:
A fee paid to exercise your option to buy (typically $200 to $400) before or at lease-end. Not included with all leases.

Rebate:
Manufacturer's money given to the customer as an incentive to purchase (lease) a specific model.

Rent Charge:
Also known as **lease fee** or **service fee.** The amount of interest you pay per month. Also known as the interest portion of your monthly lease payment.

Residual Value:
The pre-determined price of the vehicle at lease-end. The lender sets the residual value in the contract before you sign the lease. The residual value varies according to the number of months in the lease, mileage allowance, make, model, **drive-off** and **monthly lease payment** amount. May be negotiable.

Retail:
The price the general public pays for a vehicle.

Security Deposit:
100% refundable. Required by lender at time of lease signing if customer has less than a top credit rating. This fee is used to help cover costs at lease-end and is typically equal to one **monthly lease payment**. The lender can use this deposit should you fail to make a payment or damage the vehicle.

Service Fee: See **rent charge.**

Single-Payment Lease:
This is when you pay all the lease fees and monthly lease payments when you sign the contract. The advantage to this is possible savings in interest (ask your accountant) and you won't have to write a check every month.

State Fees:
May include tax, licence fee, county fee, document fee (dealer charge for doing legal paperwork), tire fee and possibly other fees.

Subsidized Lease:
This is a lease clearance sale used to move specific models quickly by lowering the **drive-off** amount and **monthly lease payments**. These subsidized leases are found in advertisements. Manufacturers offer them in place of cash **rebates** on purchased vehicles.

Sub-vented Lease: See **subsidized lease.**

Term:
Length of lease. The number of months and miles in a lease.

Termination Fee: See **disposal fee.**

Total-Due-at-Lease-Signing: See **drive-off**

Total Monthly Payment:
The amount you pay per month.

Trade-in:
Also known as **wholesale.** The price a dealer will pay for a customer's used vehicle.

Trade-in Allowance:
This is the amount the dealer will give you for your used vehicle after any existing loan or lease is paid off. Example: The dealer is willing to give you $10,000 trade-in allowance but you owe $12,000. The remaining $2,000 can be added to the price of your new vehicle lease and included in (rolled into) your monthly lease payments. You may be taxed on the trade-in ($10,000) allowance.

Wear and Usage: See **excess wear and use.**

Wear and Use: See **excess wear and use.**

Wholesale: See **trade-in.**

Window Sticker: See **Monroney Sticker.**

Window Sticker Price: See **Manufacturer's Suggested Retail Price.**

10

Before Negotiating - You Should Know

In This Chapter

The following are important areas to know before attempting to purchase or lease a new car and will help you to negotiate a car deal successfully. Being aware of the following information will allow you to get the exact car you want at the best price.

1- Dealer-to-Dealer Trade

When a customer wants to buy a car that a dealer does not have on their lot, the dealer will trade a car from their inventory with a dealer that has the car in stock.

Shipping charges may occur if the car is not local. This charge is typically passed on to the customer.

Dealer trades don't always come through on schedule. The dealer may put you off several times because they can't get the car or they're hoping you'll buy something from their inventory.

2- Factory Orders

Franchised dealerships are the only way that a customer can special order a car. You cannot order a new car directly from the manufacturer. It typically takes eight to twelve weeks from order date to delivery date. The dealer is usually willing to accept a small profit on a special-order vehicle. Negotiate with two or more dealerships for your best deal.

Incentives and rebates active on the day you take delivery should be included into the deal. Rebates active on the day you order can be yours if you get a written agreement with the dealer. To avoid any problems, it's easier if you deal with the fleet manager or sales manager and not a salesperson.

If you are trading-in your car as credit toward a factory order, obtain the dealer's offer to be paid at time of delivery in writing. When your new car comes in, the dealer cannot change their original trade-in quote unless there is obvious new damage to your car.

3- Dealer Installed Factory Add-ons

The advantage of factory add-on items is that you receive the backing of the full factory warranty. You can go to the dealership for needed repairs at no charge. These items are typically more expensive than dealer installed aftermarket add-ons.

4- Dealer Installed Aftermarket Add-ons

Aftermarket add-on items (wheels, alarm systems, etc.) are a different product than the dealer installed factory add-on product. These items have a shorter warranty period usually six months to a year and you may have to go to a shop other than the dealership for repair work. The quality of aftermarket items vary.

5- New, Demo or Pre-Owned

A car is considered new if it has never been titled, still has the full factory warranty and less than 50 to 100 test drive miles on the odometer.

A new car from the previous model year is considered new as long as the factory warranty has not been activated and the miles reflect new.

A demo or demonstrator car (also called executive unit) has been driven:

- ➤ by dealership personnel

- ➤ as a dealership rental

- ➤ on numerous test drives for potential buyers

On a demo, the factory warranty has usually been activated, bringing the car's value down. You can call the Manufacturer's Consumer Hotline Number in the Appendix to find out when the factory warranty was activated. Give them the Vehicle Identification Number (VIN) and ask them, "What's the in-service date of the factory warranty?"

A vehicle is considered pre-owned if it has been titled (owned).

6- Price Reductions:
American vs. German vs. Japanese Cars

The greatest price reductions are typically on American and Korean cars; the least on German cars. The Japanese, Swedish and English fall in between. But there are times when manufacturers of any make will need to move cars and offer great bargains. Cars of any make that are in-demand will sell for MSRP or slightly below.

7- Limited Production Cars

Limited production cars can be difficult to come by and usually bring thousands of dollars above the Manufacturer's Suggested Retail Price. These are cars that a manufacturer feeds slowly into the marketplace – usually a brand new model or a major freshening up of an existing model.

 ♦ On limited production or in-demand cars, an additional dealer mark-up will be pasted near the MSRP on the window. If you are searching for one of these cars, ask for the MSRP, then ask: "What is your window sticker price? " (dealer mark-up)

8- Maintenance Packages

This is a pre-paid plan that covers all factory scheduled maintenance requirements. These packages offered by the dealership's finance department vary in price, mileage and duration. The services typically must be done within one thousand miles (plus or minus) of your required schedule. Otherwise, you will have to pay for the service.

Obtain from the dealership's service department the factory scheduled maintenance mileage intervals and their prices from zero to 100,000 miles or the mileage limit you want. Total these prices and compare this total to the cost of the maintenance package, which is negotiable. Service departments have offer specials from time to time. Keep this in mind when negotiating. A well-negotiated maintenance package can be a great bargain.

 ♦ Make sure the local service department treats its customer and car repairs with respect. You might decide to purchase from a manufacturer that offers quality in their service department.

9- How Your Credit Affects Getting a Loan

Getting pre-qualified for a loan before you begin your car search is a good idea for people with questionable credit. Then, you can have the dealer try to beat your bank's interest rate. Otherwise, the dealer may take advantage of you with a higher interest rate.

For people with very poor credit who will have difficulty getting a loan, try your sources first (bank, credit union, family, etc.). If those sources don't pan out, find one specific dealer that is hungry and wants to work (finance) with you. The dealer will have you paying a higher interest rate and push for a higher down payment; but you can most likely still negotiate a fair amount off the MSRP. If the dealer wants to make a sale, they will do everything they can to make it happen. In a worse case scenario, you can always try to get a cosigner to sign on the contract with you. A cosigner must have good credit, be established and willing to pay on the loan if you fail to for any reason.

Important: The interest rate stated on your freshly signed contract is not locked-in until you are approved by the lender which usually takes two to ten working days. If your credit rating is questionable, the lender may want a higher interest rate. Should this happen, the dealer will notify you of the interest rate change. At this point, you have the option to sign a *new* contract at a higher interest rate, return the car and possibly pay for mileage you've driven or seek independent financing.

♦ Lending institutions are typically not available to approve a loan for a dealership on weekends and holidays.

10- How Credit Scores Work and What Credit Agencies Look At to Rate You

www.bankrate.com   5★
Gives a well rounded view of how credit ratings work and the interest rate you can expect to pay.
Click on **Auto Loans** then click on **Checking Your Credit** then click on any "Link"

www.eloan.com   5★
Explains: credit scoring, what lenders consider, how to improve your score, how to contact credit bureaus with issues.
Click on **Auto Purchase** then on right side, click on **Free credit report** then under "Free Credit Report", click on **View Sample**

www.ficoguide.com   5★
Click on "Link" of choice

11- Run Your Own Credit Report Fast

www.creditreport.com
Get your personal credit report mailed to you for a fee.

www.equifax.com
Order your credit report sent to your e-mail address for a fee.

www.ficoguide.com

www.mycreditfile.com

www.qspace.com
Explains credit scores. See your credit report online in seconds and it won't show as an inquiry.

www.transunion.com
Order and view online

12- Gap Insurance

If you are financing your car with a small down payment, consider buying gap insurance from the finance company. This insurance pays the difference between what your car insurance policy will pay and the outstanding balance on the car loan. Gap insurance protects you in case the car is totally destroyed in an accident or stolen and not found.

13- View Interest Rates & Obtain a Loan

Check with your dealership's finance department to make sure they accept checks from any of the following loan sources. If they don't, ask if they will match the offered interest rate. You can always look for your desired interest rate elsewhere.

www.bankrate.com
Click on **Auto Loans**

www.capitolone.com

www.eloan.com
View interest rates for excellent to poor credit ratings.
Click on **Auto Purchase**

www.peoplefirst.com
User friendly site for people with good credit.

www.virtualbank.com
View interest rates and monthly payments instantly.
Go to "Lending Center" then "Auto" and click on **New - Dealer**

14- Frequently Asked Questions about Getting a Loan

www.eloan.com
Click on **Auto Purchase** then on menu bar below, click on **FAQ's**
for information on loan acquisitions. Very informative.

15- Poor Credit? ... Get a Loan Here

www.carloan.com

www.carsdirect.com
Select your "Make" and "Model" then click on **Got Bad Credit?**

www.householdauto.com
Click on **Less than perfect credit?**

11

Locate and Negotiate by Phone

In This Chapter

Where This Book Came From

Buying a car can be complex but there are ways to mini-mize your effort and stress. By having proven guidelines to follow, you can now shop by telephone and bypass salespeople completely. You'll get the lowest price too!

For years, friends kept asking when I would write a book on what I do. Finally, after five years of writing, here it is. This key chapter was formed by years of experience with buying cars completely by phone.

By using the telephone, you avoid driving from dealer to dealer and enduring the "smoke and mirrors" practiced by too many salespeople. Enjoy.

1- First Things First

If you haven't read Chapters 1, 2, 4, 6 and 10, you must do so before proceeding. The information these chapters offer is necessary at this point. Without being clear of your needs in these areas, you will use your time and that of the dealership inefficiently, making them less likely to give you their best deal.

Even if you think you don't want an extended warranty, read Chapter 8 in case the finance manager succeeds in changing your mind at the last minute creating more profit for them. (They are extremely artful at doing this.) If you plan to finance, the dealership may offer you a lease at the last minute as it means more money in their pocket. Be prepared, read Chapter 9.

However, if you've read the book to this point and are feeling confident, you are now ready to locate your new car and negotiate your best deal. At this stage, you should know the year, make, model, trim level, color(s), options and packages you want and have taken the car for a test drive (optional).

You are now ready to contact dealers to find out which ones have the car you want. You will then see what deals are being offered. And finally, you will buy from the dealership that accepts your offer.

2- Where to Get Dealer Phone Numbers

Large metropolitan areas have a higher concentration of dealerships which makes for more competition and gives you a better chance of a low price.

If you live in a metropolitan area and are inclined to call three dealers, try ten instead. The more dealers you call, the better your chance of finding a dealer who is willing to sell the car far below all other dealers. It's almost like gambling; you may hit the jackpot and usually do.

If you live a distance from a metropolitan area, consider calling into the metropolitan area where the competition is better.

♦ If there are twenty dealers within the distance you are willing to travel, it's in your best interest to call every one of them.

3- Online Dealer Phone Numbers

➤ Go to www.cars.com which is the most user-friendly site for dealership phone numbers. Click on Find A Car Dealer Near You and then click on the word Distance to bring up the closest dealers first then print the list. Most dealership phone numbers, addresses and directions are found at this site.

➤ If you think the above source may have overlooked a dealer or has a wrong phone number, see Chapter 14, #42 List of Manufacturer's Website Addresses. These websites have accurate dealer phone numbers but may not be as user-friendly a site as www.cars.com.

4- Offline Dealer Phone Numbers

➤ Check your local telephone directory yellow pages, local newspapers and local auto trader magazines.

➤ Manufacturer's Consumer Hotline Numbers are found in the Appendix. Call and ask for the dealer phone numbers.

5- Fleet/Internet/Sales Manager, Salesperson - The Differences

Asking for the correct person when contacting a dealership is essential. Listed below, in order of preference are the dealership's personnel that can sell you a car.

Fleet manager - These people are the back door to the dealership and typically quote great prices right away. They have immediate knowledge as to whether a car is in stock now or will be in the near future. The fleet manager can tell you right away the various options and packages, as well as the Manufacturer's Suggested Retail Price and Dealer's Invoice price. They are the final authority in price negotiations which means no running back and forth to anyone else with your offer.

Internet manager - They are typically found at larger dealerships. They deal with customers who typically want to buy a car or get information through e-mail or by phone. This person has the same information as both the fleet and sales managers and has the same authority on price negotiations. You may experience a bit more of a sales pitch from the Internet department than with a fleet or sales manager and sometimes the Internet manager is the fleet or sales manager.

Sales manager - They have the same information as the fleet manager and can give you the same deal. Because they are in charge of a sales staff they may be more apt to try to get an extra dollar out of you.

Salesperson - Your last resort. They are the front door to the dealership and will always try to get the most money possible for a car. They generally lack access to the inventory list therefore, they must physically check the lot to see if the vehicle is in stock. This means they need your name and phone number in order to call you back at their convenience. This can be very time-consuming and frustrating.

6- Reality of Calling the Fleet or Sales Manager

It takes about an hour to call ten dealerships in order to locate the car you want. This includes gathering the necessary information such as: options, packages, exterior color, interior color and the window sticker price.

When you call a dealership and ask for the fleet manager, you are usually connected quickly. But in some instances, you may not get through because they are busy. The following is a guide that will help you get connected to a manager.

On your first call:

> If you are put on hold by the receptionist longer than you like, hang up and hit redial. Calling back will usually get you quicker results.

> If you get the fleet manager's voice mail, keep in mind they may not return your call for several hours or a day. If you want speedy results, call back a little later.

If you must make a second call, ask the receptionist: *"Could you tell me the name of the fleet manager on duty at the moment?"* Why should you say "at the moment?" Because it gets the message across to the receptionist to pay attention to who is on duty presently. There may be several fleet managers that work at a dealership on different shifts. If you are told their first name only, get their last name too, then ask to be connected. If you don't get through on this call, you should call other dealerships on your list before trying this dealership again. The next time you call this dealership, ask for the fleet manager by their first and last name.

In case a third call is needed, ask the receptionist: *"Could you tell me if Joe Smith is available at the moment?"* If the receptionist responds "okay" you are now being transferred to Joe Smith the fleet manager. If you don't get through to Joe Smith on this call, you should hang up, hit redial, and ask the receptionist: *"Do you know if a fleet or sales manager is available? I need to talk to someone in person. Is anyone available as we speak?"* The receptionist will then try to connect you to an available manager. It's extremely rare to not get a manager by the third call. If you haven't, it's time to ask for a salesperson. You will only be asking the salesperson if your specific car is on their lot. Nothing else.

7- Your Last Resort: The Salesperson

At times, a dealership can be so busy (typically Friday evening or Saturday) you cannot reach a fleet or sales manager. Unless you want to wait until a manager is available, you'll have to ask for a salesperson.

1. After you say hello and introduce yourself to the salesperson ask: *"Do you have a pen and paper available to write down what I'm looking for?"* If they don't, ask them to get a pen and paper so you don't have to repeat yourself several times.

2. Once the salesperson is ready, tell him or her what you want. For example: *"Do you have a 2005 Honda Accord LX, four-door, automatic with a white exterior in stock right now?"* It's best not to go into the small details like CD, chrome wheels, tinted windows, etc. at this time because after all, they may not have the car on the lot and this would be

very time consuming.

3. The salesperson will ask for your name and phone number. Before you give it, ask: *"How long before you can call me back?"* You should get this answered before giving your phone number. The salesperson could be off to another deal and possibly forget to call you back. After negotiating a time frame of thirty minutes or less, give the salesperson your phone number. Also, get his or her first and last name in case you need to call them.

4. If the salesperson doesn't call as agreed upon, call the dealership and ask for the salesperson by their full name. When you get the person on the phone say: *"Hi, this is so-and-so, do you have the car I asked for on your lot?"*

If the salesperson did not get the information, your current call will jolt them into action and they will most likely have the information for you within ten to twenty minutes.

When the salesperson calls back, if he or she doesn't have the car on their lot, don't let them keep you on the phone by saying they can do a dealer trade or that the car is on the way. This dealership simply doesn't have the car you want. Move on.

The exception to this rule is if you are seeking a rare car. Then ask them if the specific car will be coming in and when. Ask for the Vehicle Identification Number as they have that before the arrival of the vehicle.

If the salesperson says the dealership has the car on their lot, (or they have your rare car coming in) write down all the information you want and say: *"Thank you for your help. Let me decide what I need to do at this time."* Politely get off the phone.

8- Keep or Drop the Salesperson?

If you found your car through a salesperson and you're inclined to keep them as your main contact, keep in mind it will most likely be more time consuming and more costly than if you went through a manager. The salesperson will ask for more money than either the fleet or sales manager would accept because that's their job.

If you prefer a quicker and easier approach to your purchase or lease with a much better chance for a lower price, call back and ask the receptionist for the fleet manager. When you get the manager on the phone, ask them to look at their inventory list for the car you want. They will see that they have it and you can now proceed with negotiations. You don't need to tell them you called previously or that you know the car is on their lot. In the unlikely event the manager found out you called earlier, it wouldn't be an issue because they want your business.

♦ Don't ask the salesperson to transfer you to a manager because they will most likely tell you why you should stay with them and ultimately interfere with your deal.

9- Watch Out for Salespeople Pretending to Be a Manager

During regular business hours (9am to 6pm Monday through Friday) your chances of being connected to a fleet or sales manager are very good. To save time, simply say: "Fleet department please." There are numerous fleet managers at some dealerships and you want to be connected to one that is available.

Three possible ways to tell if a salesperson is pretending to be a manager:

1. When the receptionist transfers you to a fleet or sales manager, ask: *"Are you the fleet or sales manager?"* Any answer but a straight *"Yes"* might be a salesperson taking the business.

2. When the receptionist transfers you to a fleet or sales manager and you hear a *sales pitch* (see Sales Talk below), it is probably a salesperson. Hang up, hit redial and ask the receptionist for the fleet or sales manager's first and last name, then ask to be connected. When your call is answered, ask with whom you are speaking. If they are not who you called for, ask for the person you want by name. Fortunately, this rarely happens.

3. After 6pm Monday through Friday, the receptionist has probably gone for the day. There is a good chance that when you call, a salesperson will answer the phone. To by-pass this hazard, the first thing you

should do is ask for the first and last name of the sales manager on duty at the moment (few fleet managers work into the late evening). After you have the name of the sales manager, ask to be connected. When your call is answered, ask with whom you are speaking. If they are not who you called for, ask again for the person you want by name.

10- Sales Talk

A type of conversation salespeople use in order to create confusion and a sale as quickly as possible. It generally creates upset or stress to varying levels in the person it's aimed at.

Sales talk can sound like the following:

> ➤ When can you come in?

> ➤ I can't give out quotes over the phone. Can we make an appointment for you to come in?

> ➤ What would it take to put you into this car today?

> ➤ We have great deals happening today, are you ready to buy?

> ➤ We have plenty of cars like you want, can we make an appointment for you to come in this afternoon?

> ➤ How much are you willing to spend?

> ➤ Will you be leasing or financing?

Fleet managers are usually direct and do not use sales talk. For example, they will say something like: "Let me check. Yes, we have one." or "No, we don't have one but I can get it for you."

11- Sample Call

This sample call section is for reading purposes only. The following are the steps you will need to take in order to get the information you want by phone.

Very important: If you are not brief and to-the-point in your questioning with the fleet or sales manager, you may be passed on to a salesperson.

Do not make small talk on your first call and this won't happen. If there's a pause in the conversation, stay quiet. If they ask you a question, answer it briefly and professionally. These managers are very busy and do not have time to chit chat, at least not on your first call. If it turns out they have the car you want at the price you like, you will then have plenty of time to talk freely and become buddies if you like.

☞   You will need Calling Guide #1 (at the end of this chapter) as a format and a notebook to write in. Give yourself lots of note space, you'll probably need it.

1. Call a dealership on your list (see #2 "Where to Get Dealer Phone Numbers" in this chapter) and say to the receptionist: *"Fleet manager please."* When the fleet manager says "hello", you immediately say: *"Do you have a (for example) 2005 Honda Accord LX, four-door, automatic with a black exterior in stock right now?"* Adding the words right now makes it clear you're looking for a car they have in stock on their lot and not a dealer trade. Inquire about the interior color, CD, tinted windows and special options later.

The fleet manager will look over the inventory list. Let's assume the car is in stock. The fleet manager will say: "Yes, I have one."

2. Verify the year again. Sometimes the manager will be thinking "new," which may include the previous end-of-year model. Verifying the year is done because the current model year could be a new body style with added features whereas last year's model is still brand new, but depreciated. Then ask: *"What options and packages does it have that add to the base price of the car?"* Make sure you say: that add to the base price of the car clearly, otherwise they will likely give you standard features that come with all cars at no extra charge and this will not be a good use of time for either party.

Ask the price for each option and package separately and write them down.

3. Next ask: *"What's the window sticker price?"* (Manufacturer's Suggested Retail Price - defined in Chapter 9, #17 "Leasing Glossary.")

4. Then ask: *"How much from dealer's invoice* (what the dealer pays for a car) *can you let me have the car for?"* Experience shows,

more often than not, they will give you a price quote. If they don't give you a price quote, you'll get the manager to respond to an offer you will make later. This is explained in #12 "Calculating Your First Purchase Offer" in this chapter.

♦ The word <u>from</u> is used because they can sell a car above or below dealer's invoice. If you use the word <u>above</u>, they will think you're an amateur and probably quote you a higher price.

Important: The Dealer's Invoice is the only price to focus on and the only way you will ever know just how good of a deal you are getting. The <u>out the door</u> price leads you to think you're getting a great deal when in fact you're usually not. You need to know how much above or below Dealer's Invoice you are paying in order to compare one deal to another. This way, you'll know exactly how good or bad a dealer's quote is.

5. If the fleet manager gives you a price quote, ask: *"What's the dealer's invoice price on the car?"* Repeat this question until you get the figure and write it down. This is the best time to get this important information, so make sure you try to get the figure.

♦ There is a difference between <u>dealer's invoice</u> and <u>dealer's cost</u>. If the dealer says the word <u>cost</u> instead of <u>invoice</u>, it will be a higher price. Get the dealer to tell you the dealer's <u>invoice</u> amount.

☞ You can also go to <u>www.kbb.com</u> to get the dealer's invoice on the car. If there's a discrepancy between what the dealer tells you and the price on <u>www.kbb.com</u>, ask the dealer to explain exactly where the difference lies.

☞ Most dealers will answer question #4 and #5. If they do not, you'll see how to make them an offer later. If you are leasing, you need to go to #17 "Getting the First Lease Quote from a Dealer" in this chapter now. If you are purchasing or financing, see #6 below.

6. By this point, you should know of any factory-to-customer cash rebate, incentive or low interest rates and have written them in your notebook. Verify this information with the manager you have on the phone.

Ask only two dealers this question. If there are no special interest rates, ask: *"What is the current interest rate, assuming I have good credit?"* Ask only two dealers these questions.

7. You have now completed your first call. Keep going, call every dealer on your list and follow the same format. Don't be tempted to take the easy way out and accept an early dealer's best price quote. The feeling you will have after calling all the dealers on your list and knowing exactly where the cars are is very empowering. With this knowledge, you will negotiate with much more confidence. And remember, there could be that one special dealer out there who wants to give you a great deal.

Sometimes there is only one dealer that has a car that matches your criteria. For instance, you want a white car and only one dealer on your list has the car. Before making an offer, call another dealer and negotiate on a car of a different color. If you negotiate with more than one dealer, you can use this information as a basis for your first real offer on the actual car you want.

12- Calculating Your First Purchase Offer

The following steps will help you calculate your first offer:

1. Readily available cars can usually be purchased for $100 to $500 over dealer's invoice. Dealer's invoice is what the dealer pays the manufacturer for a car, not the Manufacturer's Suggested Retail Price (MSRP) which is substantially higher. The amount you can negotiate off the price of a car varies. The greatest price reductions are typically on American cars; the least on German cars. The Japanese fall in between. But there are times when manufacturers of any make will need to move cars and offer great bargains.

Cars that are in-demand will sell for MSRP or slightly below. Your initial price quotes from dealers will tell you if the car you want fits in this category.

Rare or limited production cars can be priced above MSRP. These are cars that a manufacturer feeds slowly into the marketplace – usually a brand new model or a major freshening up of an existing model.

Whatever the case, the price you begin negotiating from is the dealer's marked-up window sticker price which is higher than the MSRP.

2. Use the lowest price quote you received as your initial guide. For example, an MSRP of $23,000 might have a Dealer's Invoice price of $20,000. Let's say the lowest dealer quote was $200 over invoice, which equals $20,200.

3. Deduct the full factory-to-dealer incentive (if any) from this price (example: dealer quoted price, $20,200 minus a $1,000 dealer incentive equals $19,200).

☞ If any of your dealer price quotes are below the dealer's invoice, the manager may be deducting some or all of their manufacturer-to-dealer incentive money already. Some eager managers will give you their absolute lowest price quote immediately (for dealer incentives, see Chapter 6, "Dealers' Hidden Profits").

4. If you want to get the very best price possible, reduce your offer depending upon the initial dealer quotes. Your reduction on a car with a dealer's invoice of $20,000 might be $1,000 below dealer's invoice price or $2,000 to $5,000 below invoice on a $50,000 car. At times there are special factory bonuses, typically for end-of-month or especially end-of-quarter purchases. Offering a reduced price might uncover a factory bonus.

♦ **You want to discover what price reduction is possible but not turn off the dealer and have them hang up on you. Don't go too low with your offer.**

5. Factory-to-customer cash rebates are deducted only after you and the manager have agreed on a vehicle price (see Chapter 3, Best Times of Year to Buy).

☞ If you would like the bulk of the dealer's profit knocked off quickly without having to calculate an offer, go to Chapter 14, #17 "View Bargain Prices You Can Offer a Dealer." But keep in mind, you won't get the absolute rock bottom price that you would by negotiating among several dealers.

♦ On a 0 down, 0 interest and 0 payments for the first year finance, ask the dealer what your interest rate will be when you begin making your payments a year from now. (It may change from 0% to 10% or more).

13- Making the Offer While Testing the Market for Price

Once you've located which dealers have the car of your choice, you are ready to make your first offer. You should know the following information:

➤ Options and packages that add to the base price of the car

➤ The window sticker price

➤ Dealer quotes and Dealer's Invoice prices are helpful to have

Call the contact person that gave you the lowest price and say: *"I'd like to make an offer and if you accept my offer, I can be at your dealership to pick up the car by* (example: 5pm) *today."* You need to let them know that you are an immediate and serious buyer for them to give you their best price.

The manager usually says: "Okay, what's your offer?"

Ask the following questions one at a time and get a clear response to each item.

1. *"Will you fill the gas tank on this new car?"* The typical response is "yes".

2. *"Will you have the vehicle freshly detailed before I pick it up?"* This service is supposed to be done on a new vehicle, but is not always done. You want a "yes" response.

3. *"I would like the floor mats included in my offer, is that okay?"* Floor mats don't always come standard with a new car. Have them included. They should say "yes" without a problem.

Then you can say:

4. *"I'll give you $X dollars."* (your calculated amount from #12

"Calculating Your First Purchase Offer" in this chapter).

♦ **Once you make your first offer, negotiations will go quickly.**

They may respond: "That's lower than I can go."

You say:

5. *"How close to my offer can you come?"*

They will usually give their lowest or close to lowest price quote at this point.

Write it down and say:

6. *"Okay, let me think about it and I'll call you back shortly."*

Call all the other dealerships that have the car you want on their lot even if they didn't give you a price quote earlier. Follow the above example and make them your offer.

If the manager accepts your first calculated offer, you may have offered too high. Say:

7. *"Okay, let me decide what I need to do. Thank you for your help."* Politely hang-up. The reason they may have accepted your first offer could have been because you miscalculated in their favor. Recalculate your offer and call the other dealers with your new offer then call the first dealer again.

♦ **Never mention competing dealers until you are negotiating with the final two. Even then, mention competitors only if necessary and never say which dealer or town specifically. This can cause unnecessary tension between you and the dealer.**

♦ **A today buyer will most likely get a better deal than a tomorrow buyer.**

♦ **If you want factory or dealer installed add-on items or an extended warranty, now is the time to negotiate these items.**

☞ For negotiating a finance or purchase, use Calling Guide #1 and #2 at the end of this chapter.

14- Negotiating the Extended Warranty

The best time to get the lowest price on an extended warranty is after negotiating the price of your new car. Ask the manager:

1. *"If I buy this vehicle for our agreed upon price, will you sell me* (for example) *the Platinum Plus* (be specific on the warranty name), *7-year, 100,000 mile warranty* (year and mileage terms), *with $0 deductible for $X dollars?"*

Start by offering a little less than half of the finance managers quoted retail price. Example: $2,000 retail price, offer $900.

The manager may say "no" to your offer.

2. If so ask: *"How close to my offer can you come?"*

Get the manager to commit to a price by asking this question until you get a price. The manager may respond with, "$1,300."

3. You can then say: *"If you can do it for $1,000 it's a deal."*

The manager may say: "$1,200 is the best I can do."

4. If you choose to continue negotiations, say: *"$1,100 is my maximum."*

The manager may say: "That's fine, let's do it."

If you and the manager do not come to an agreed upon price, call a different dealership that has the next best negotiated car price and negotiate the warranty to see if you can get it for a price you like.

♦ **Experience shows that the dealer selling a car at the best price will usually sell extras at the best price too.**

☞ For negotiating an extended warranty, use Calling Guide #4 at the end of this chapter.

15- Negotiating Factory or Aftermarket Add-ons

Factory and dealer aftermarket add-on items (CD, chrome wheels, etc.) are marked-up approximately 30 percent from wholesale. Begin negotiations by offering the wholesale price (about 70% of retail). Example: On your calculator, retail price times 30 percent, then hit the minus button for wholesale price. Keep in mind that factory or dealer aftermarket add-ons are typically not factory options or packages.

　　☞　For negotiating factory or aftermarket add-ons, negotiate in the manner stated in Calling Guide #4, "Negotiating an Extended Warranty" at the end of this chapter.

16- Negotiating Your Interest Rate

If there are no factory sponsored low interest rates being offered or your credit doesn't allow you to receive them, the following information will show you how to negotiate your interest rate.

　　☞　If your credit rating is not top notch, you might want to see Chapter 10, #9 "How Your Credit Affects Getting a Loan."

One of the best times to negotiate an interest rate is **after** you have completed your first round of offers and have an idea of the current interest rates. Then call the contact person you think you are most likely going to buy from and ask:

　　1. *"What is the current interest rate on a* (choose one or more: 36, 48, 60, 72) *month loan?"*

They will most likely reply: "What's your credit rating?"

Unless you know your credit rating is poor, you should say:

　　2. *"It's perfect, and if for any reason you find it lacking, I'm aware that the interest rate will go up."*

　　♦ **The above statement lets the manager know you are reasonable and usually convinces them to give you an interest rate quote.**

For example, your contact person will then generally respond: "It's 6 percent right now."

You should answer:

　　3. *"If you can do it for 4 percent, you have a deal."* Take charge

and make this a statement, not a question.

The manager may counter with: "Let's do it for 5 percent."

If you're inclined to continue negotiations, make another offer or say: *"Let me think about it and I may call you back later. Thank you for your help."* Call the next dealer you are most likely to buy from and negotiate the interest rate. This process only needs to be done with one or two dealers.

Another best time to negotiate is **immediately after** the dealer quotes you an interest rate based on your credit check.

    ☞   The credit check process is covered in detail in Chapter 12, "Finalizing The Deal."

If your credit check shows some problems, the interest rate will be higher but you can still try to negotiate this higher rate to something lower.

For example, the dealer may tell you: "The best I can do is 10 percent."

You should reply:

    1. *"If you can do it for 8.5 percent, you have a deal."* Again, make this a statement, not a question.

They may answer: "I'll do it for 9.5."

If you're still not satisfied and want to continue negotiations, make another offer. Or you can say:

    2. *"I need to think about it, I'll call you back later."* Saying this might make them nervous enough to give you the interest rate you want. Again, you won't need to do this process with more than one or two dealers.

    ☞   For negotiating your interest rate, use Calling Guide #3 at the end of this chapter.

17- Getting the First Lease Quote from a Dealer

Ask the first dealer that has the car you want:

    1. *"How much is the drive-off amount* (total-due-at-lease-signing)

and monthly lease payment without tax on a (for example*) three-year,
12,000-mile per year lease?"* If you want options such as mats, CD,
chrome wheels, etc. added to the car, make sure you tell your contact
person to include these items into the lease.

The dealer may ask: "What's your credit like?"

Unless you know your credit rating is poor, you can reply:

2. *"It's perfect and if for any reason you find it lacking, I'm
aware the numbers will go up."*

3. Also ask: *"How long before you can call back with the numbers?"*

The manager will usually tell you: "Thirty minutes or so."

While you are waiting for this dealer to get back, continue your calls to
the rest of the dealers on your list to find which ones have the car and
with what options, packages and the window sticker prices.

4. If there's no response from the first manager after a half an hour
or so, call your contact person and ask: *"Have you had a chance to
calculate the drive-off amount and monthly lease payment yet?"* If
they still don't have the numbers for you, this will be a reminder for them
to crunch your numbers. Ask again: *"How long before you will call
back?"*

Keep calling other dealers while waiting for the first dealer's crunched
numbers or if thirty minutes goes by, you should call this dealer back.

When you finally get the crunched numbers, make sure the dealer's
monthly lease payment does not include tax.

This first lease quote is your starting point for negotiating.

♦ There are time-consuming details involved in getting a lease
   quote. One quote is all that is needed to get started.

18- Preparing to Make a Lease Offer

At this time, you must decide what you want your total-due-at-lease-
signing (drive-off) to be. Decide on an amount that you are financially

comfortable with (Example: $0, $1,000, $3,000) and don't ever change it during negotiations so you can negotiate the monthly lease payment only.

You must **never** change this total-due-at-lease-signing amount during negotiations with any dealer. A dealer could easily confuse you when working with two variables such as the total-due-at-lease-signing and the monthly lease payment.

♦ **Even if you negotiate a price substantially below the window sticker price, a dealer can still include extra fees into your monthly lease payment. This cannot happen if you negotiate the monthly lease payment alone.**

Now continue to call the rest of the dealers on your list to locate which ones have the car you want on their lot.

Hopefully, you won't be tempted to take the easy way out and begin negotiating at this point. The feeling you will have after calling all the dealers on your list and knowing exactly where these cars are is extremely empowering. With this knowledge (where the cars are) you will negotiate with much more confidence. And remember, there could be that one dealer that needs to move one more car in order to receive a large incentive and will give you a great deal.

Once you have located which dealers have the car and you know the options, packages and the window sticker price, you are ready to call them back with an offer.

The initial quote you received from your first call is all that is necessary to determine what your first offer should be.

19- Making the Lease Offer

Call a contact person from the list of dealers that has the car you want and say:

1. *"I'd like to make an offer on the car."* (Make this offer to the dealer who gave you the initial quote too at some point.)

A manager's typical response is: "What do you have in mind?"

Your offer should be 30 percent less than the initial monthly lease payment quote you received earlier. If your chosen drive-off amount is substantially below the initial quote (example: it was $3,000, your limit is $1,000) this $2,000 reduction will automatically be applied to and raise your monthly payments. Therefore, you should reduce your monthly payment offer by 20 percent instead of 30 percent.

Ask the manager:

2. *"If I lease this car today, will you include a full tank of gas and a fresh detail?"*

The manager should say "yes."

At this point, mention the options (example: mats, chrome wheels, CD, etc.) you want.

Tell the manager:

3. *"I will give you $X dollars* (example: $1,000) *at lease signing and $X dollars a month plus tax* (30 percent less than the first dealer's initial quote) *on* (as an example) *a three-year, 12,000-mile lease. If you agree to this, I will pick it up by 5pm."*

The manager may say: "What's your credit rating like?"

Unless you know your credit is poor, say:

4. *"It's perfect and if you accept my offer, I'm willing to let you do a credit check. If for any reason you find my credit is lacking, I'm aware that the monthly lease payment will go up. Do you accept my offer?"*

The manager's typical response is: "I can do $X (higher than your offer) dollars a month."

Caution: In rare instances (possibly due to a misunderstanding), the dealer may increase the total-due-at-lease-signing to meet your monthly payment offer. If this happens, tell them your original drive-off amount must not change and have them redo the monthly lease payment.

Then say:

5. *"Is that the closest you can come to my offer?"*

The manager will usually give you their lowest price at this point.

You ask:

6. *"Is the tax included in your monthly payment quote?"* If it is, ask them for a payment quote without the tax. This will make it much easier to follow all the dealer quotes.

Then you say:

7. *"Okay, let me think about it and I'll call you back shortly."*

Now, follow the above example with all the dealerships that have your car in stock.

If no dealer accepts your first monthly payment offer, your offer is too low. If you want to negotiate further with one or more of the lowest priced dealers, raise your offer 30 percent of the difference. For example, your offer is $300 and the dealer's lowest quote is $400. There is a $100 difference. Thirty percent of $100 is $30. ($30 plus $300 equals $330). Make the dealer an offer of $330.

Call a contact person and say:

8. *"If you let me have the car for $330 a month plus tax I will be in at 5pm to pick up the car."*

The manager may come down in price but not meet your offer. At this point you can lease the car or continue negotiations.

☞ For negotiating a lease, use Calling Guide #1 and #5 at the end of this chapter.

20- How to Get Lower Payments on a Lease Special

A lease special is also known as a subsidized lease by dealers. A manufacturer will offer these to the consumer in order to move certain models quickly. They are easily found in advertisements or you can ask the dealer if any special leases are currently being offered on the model of interest. These special leases have a lower total-due-at-lease-signing and lower monthly lease payments than regular lease prices.

Without mentioning an advertisement you saw, offer the dealer a lower drive-off amount (25 percent less) and a lower monthly payment (10 percent less) than the advertised prices.

The manager may quote you a price lower than the advertised prices but higher than your offer.

You are doing great by beating a subsidized lease offer. If you are inclined to continue negotiations make another offer.

21- Calling Guides

The following Calling Guides can be used either as a reference from which you make notations in a notebook or by **photo copying** these original guides as many times as needed. You can enlarge the book's Calling Guide on a copy machine.

1. Start by writing the name of the city where the dealership is located.

2. Call this dealership and if they don't have the car you want, write or circle "NO" and call the next dealership.

3. If they have the car you want, follow the Calling Guide and write your notes accordingly.

Calling Guide #1

Gathering Information for:
Purchase/Finance/Lease

Pre-call Information

Customer Cash Rebate $_____ or _____% (see Chapter 3)

Dealer Incentive $_____ (see Chapter 6)

Subsidized lease price: drive-off $_____

Monthly lease payment $_____

---

1. Dealership Location _____

2. Phone # _____

3. Contact Person _____

4. Dealership Name_____

Specific questions to ask the manager:

5. "Do you have a:

Year _____   Make _____

Model _____   Trim level _____

2 / 4 door_____   auto/manual_____

exterior color _____   in stock right now?"   YES   NO

6. "What's the window sticker price on the car?" $_____

7. "What options or packages does this car have **that add to the base price**?" _____   _____   _____

8. "How much are each of these items?" _____   _____   _____

9. "How much **from** dealer's invoice can you let me have the car for?" $_____

Calling Guide #1 ...continued

10. "What's the Dealer's Invoice on the car?" $_____
(Make sure they say dealer's <u>invoice</u> and not dealer's <u>cost</u>.)
Most dealers will answer question #9 and #10. If they do not, you'll see how to make them an offer later.

If you are leasing, go to "Calling Guide #5 - Negotiating a Lease" now. If you are purchasing or financing, go to #11 below.

11. Verify your factory-to-customer cash rebate or special interest rates (36 month)_____% (48 month)_____% (60 month)_____%
(ask 2 dealers only)

12. "What is the current interest rate assuming I have great credit?"
_____% (ask 2 dealers only)

Repeat steps #1 through #10 with all the dealers on your list before making any offer then go to "Calling Guide #2" and follow the steps.

Calling Guide #2

Negotiating a Purchase or Finance

To help you decide on your initial offer (cash or finance), go to #12 "Calculating Your First Purchase Offer" in this chapter. You will then be ready to make your first purchase offer by using the following steps.

First Purchase Offer

1. Before making your first offer, make sure the fleet or sales manager says yes to the following: "I would like a full tank of gas, fresh detail and floor mats. Will you include these into my offer?"

2. Write your first offer above or below dealers invoice on the line in #3 below.
(Example: If Dealer's Invoice is $20,000 and you offer $300 above it, write $20,300 on this line.)

3. Say: "If you accept $_____ (for example $20,300) plus state fees, I'll pick it up by _____ am / pm."
OR "I'll give you (for example) $300 (above or below) dealers invoice and I'll pick it up by _____ am / pm."
(State fees are non-negotiable; they are always in addition to the negotiated price of the car.)

4. If the dealer does not accept your offer, ask: "How close to my offer can you come?" Write down the dealer's closest price quote to your offer. $_____

5. You respond: "Let me think about it and I will call you back."

Repeat steps 1 through 5 with the dealers that have the car on their lot.

If you are happy with the lowest offer you received after calling all the dealers and want to buy the car, go to Chapter 12, "Finalizing the Deal." If not, continue with your second offer.

Calling Guide #2 ...continued

Second Purchase Offer

Call the 1 or 2 best priced dealer(s) you want to further negotiate with.

6. Write your second offer $_____ (higher than your first offer)

7. Say: "If you accept (written offer amount) plus state fees, I'll pick it up by ___ am / pm."

If you come to an agreement, go to Chapter 12, "Finalizing the Deal." If not, continue on.

8. If the dealer does not accept your offer, ask: "How close to my offer can you come?" Write down the dealer's closest price quote to your offer. $_____

9. You respond: "Let me think about it and I will call you back."

Repeat steps 6 through 8 with the last dealer.

10. Continue negotiations or pick the dealer with the best quote and go to Chapter 12, "Finalizing the Deal."

This is the time to negotiate factory or dealer installed add-on items such as: chrome wheels, CD, alarm or an extended warranty (see Calling Guide #4 as a negotiating format).

Calling Guide #3

Negotiating an Interest Rate

Ask your contact person (for example):

1. "What's the current interest rate on a 48 or 60 month loan assuming I have great credit? If you find my credit lacking for any reason, I'm aware the rate will go up." Write the interest rate on the line below.

Dealer's quoted interest rate _____ %

Your **first** interest rate offer:

2. "Can you do it for_____% ?" (lower than dealer's quote)

Dealer's counter offer _____% (same as or lower than their first quote)

If you're still not satisfied, continue below.

Your **second** interest rate offer:

3. "If you do it for _____% you have a deal." (same as or higher than your first offer)

Dealer's counter offer _____% (same as or lower than their counter offer)

After you agree on an interest rate with a dealer, go to Chapter 12, "Finalizing the Deal."

Calling Guide #4

Negotiating an Extended Warranty

By this point, you need to have the retail price of the warranty from your contact person and write it on this line $_____

Ask your contact person:

1. "If I buy this vehicle for our agreed upon price, will you sell me the (example below):

- ➤ Platinum Plus (be specific on the warranty name)
- ➤ 7-year, 100,000-mile warranty (year and mileage terms)
- ➤ with $0 deductible for $_____ (dollars) ?"

Offer less than half of your contact person's quoted retail price. Example: $2,000 retail price, offer $900.

If the manager says "no" to your offer, ask:

2. "How close to my offer can you come?"

Write their response $_____ (a price higher than your offer)

You can then say:

3. "If you sell it to me for $_____ you have a deal." (a bit higher than your first offer)

Your contact person may say: "$_____ is the best I can do." (the same as or a bit lower than their first quote)

If you choose to continue negotiations, say:

4. "$_____ and it's a done deal." (the same as or a bit higher than your last offer)

The manager may say: "That's fine, let's do it."

If you haven't come to an agreed upon price, call the dealership with the next best car price to negotiate the warranty.

Calling Guide #5

Negotiating a Lease

This Guide shows monthly lease payments with tax excluded. Insist that the dealer keep the tax out of the monthly payment to eliminate all possible confusion. You add taxes onto your monthly lease payment only after negotiations are finalized.

1. Ask: "What is the drive-off amount and monthly lease payment without tax on a (for example) 3 year, 12,000 mile lease?" Dealer's quoted drive-off amount $_____ and monthly payment $_____ without tax.

2. If the drive-off amount is other than what you want, choose a drive-off amount that you are comfortable with and NEVER allow your contact person to change this amount (lower drive-off's require better credit ratings). You never want to negotiate both, your drive-off amount and your monthly lease payment; you have to lock one in. If you permit your contact person to work with both numbers, they can get the upper hand in negotiations. Write in your chosen drive-off amount $_____ (example: $0, $1,000, $3,000).

3. Say: "If I lease this car from you today, will you include a full tank of gas, mats and a fresh detail?" (Get a yes on all three before going on.)

4. If you want other options included, say: "I also want (example: chrome wheels, CD, etc.) included into my lease."

5. Say: "I want my monthly lease payment to be based on a (for example) three-year, 12,000 mile per year lease."

6. Say: "I will give you $_____ drive-off (example: $1,000) and $_____ a month (30 percent less than initial dealer quote) plus tax. If you agree to this, I'll pick the car up by ____ am / pm."

7. If the dealer doesn't accept your offer, say: "How close to my offer can you come?" Dealer's monthly payment quote $_____ tax not included. Make sure the dealer hasn't changed your chosen drive-off amount and if they did, have them re-do the numbers.

Calling Guide #5 ...continued

Repeat steps 1 thru 7 with all the dealers that have the car on their lot.

8. You can now pick the dealer with the best price quote and go to Chapter 12, "Finalizing the Deal" or continue negotiations as stated below.

9. Choose one or more of the best priced dealers and raise your offer by 30%. Example: Your offer is $300 and the best dealer quote is $400. There is a $100 difference. 30% of $100 equals $30. Offer $330.

10. Say: "I'll give you $_____ a month plus tax."

11. If the dealer does not accept your offer, say: "How close to my offer can you come?" Dealer's closest quote $_____ tax not included.

12. Once you have their new quote, say: "Okay, let me think about it and I'll call you back shortly."

13. Pick the dealer with the best quote and go to Chapter 12, "Finalizing the Deal."

12

Finalizing The Deal

In This Chapter

Whether you are buying your car through an Online Car Buying Service or by phone, you should not go to the dealership to pick up your new car until you have negotiated every potential aspect of the deal. Negotiating anything on the car lot puts you at a *severe* disadvantage; therefore, following the information in this chapter will help you to avoid all potential pitfalls.

You've done great to this point. Don't make a mistake now. The dealer still has countless ways of extracting more money out of your deal in very unexpected ways. Hold steady and follow along to finalize your deal by phone.

If you don't already know the following information, call your contact person at the dealership and ask the following in order to verify that the car is physically on their lot:

- ➤ Year

- ➤ Make, model

- ➤ Trim level (base model versus luxury model)

- ➤ Options (such as: CD player) and packages (such as: leather and moonroof) that add to the base price of the car

- ➤ Manufacturer's Suggested Retail Price

- ➤ Exterior and interior color

1- Odometer Reading

By phone, ask your contact person:

"How many miles does the car have on the odometer?" The dealer must physically go out to the car and look at the odometer and then call you with the mileage. This assures the car is absolutely on the dealership's lot.

If there are more miles on the car than you like, you may still be able to negotiate the price or go after another car with less miles.

A new car typically has less than ten miles on the odometer. If the car has more than 50 to 100 miles on it, ask how the miles were put on. Test drive miles may be OK but anything else is cause for renegotiation.

2- Maybe They Will Fax Some Paperwork

The Dealer's Invoice is a blue print of a cars make-up and will tell you everything about the car.

Have the dealer fax you the Dealer's Invoice. If they hesitate, it's probably because they are concerned that you will use the information to negotiate for another car with another dealer. If need be, tell them you won't do that.

If they still won't fax the Dealer's Invoice, ask for the Vehicle Identification Number (VIN). There's no reason for the dealer to withhold the VIN.

Ask the dealer to fax you a finished contract or some form of paperwork that outlines the terms of the deal.

Try to have the dealer hold your car by putting a credit card deposit (typically $200 to $1,000) on it. If the dealer says that they will hold the car for you without a credit card deposit they usually will, but then again, it's possible they may not. If you don't want to risk them selling it to someone else for more profit, you will have to go to the dealership and buy or lease the car as soon as possible, usually that day.

3- Dealing With The Finance Manager

You will be doing the paperwork (contract, etc.) with the best salesperson the dealership has on staff; the finance manager. Pay attention to this fact because they make a commission on what they sell you. They're extremely good at bringing in much more money for a dealership than the profit made on the sale of a new car. And this is all done with a very believable face . If you haven't done your research on the items they offer, chances are, they will convince you that you need it. Your only defense is doing good research before going in. Without proper research, you'll probably overpay for anything you buy and not ever know it.

♦ **The finance department is a well oiled money making machine.**

Warning: Don't walk into the finance room unprepared, do your research before going in.

The following are high-profit items the finance manager will offer you:

➤ Extended warranty

➤ Rust proofing - if you don't live where there is salt or snow on the streets in the winter, you don't need it.

➤ Paint sealant - your local detailer will do just as good a job for less than one third the price.

➤ Scotch guard fabric protection - take it to your detailer for a much better price.

➤ Alarm system - check with your local auto alarm store. They may offer a better overall value.

➤ Window etching (VIN engraved on windows) - a local engraver can do it much cheaper or simply don't buy it.

➤ Keyless entry - It's a great option. Check local pricing and compare.

➤ LoJac - if your car is stolen, the police can track and possibly find it. Your insurance rate may be lowered if you have one or you can let your insurance cover the lose if the car is stolen. Ask whether your car comes equipped with a factory-installed tracking device.

➤ Credit life/disability/accidental health insurance - covers your car payments in the event you are incapacitated for a period of time. Your insurance company, credit union or bank will most likely have a substantially better rate than the dealer.

Call and ask the finance manager : "What items, add-ons or packages do you have to offer?" With this information, you can do your pricing research ahead of time and decide what you do and don't want before going into the dealership. They may not want to give this information up easily because they know they have a better chance at a larger profit if you are sitting across the desk from them. Go over the list above and ask until you're sure they've told you every single thing they offer and there is nothing more they can make a big profit on. Also, ask how long the warranty is on any add-on item that you might be interested in .

Negotiate these items over the phone or you could get pressured into paying double or triple the price than you would elsewhere.

The dealership may offer factory items (CD, roof rack, etc.) that are covered under the full factory warranty. The convenience of going to the dealership for warranty repairs on these items may be worth the added premium. Also, any additional add-on costs (well-negotiated of course) can be included into your monthly payment. Purchase of an add-on from an outside source will require a separate check for the total amount.

◆ You may want to call the parts department directly to verify the item to be installed is in stock. If there is an item that needs to be installed at a future date, make sure you negotiate to have a loaner car available when you drop off your new car.

4- Know the Numbers

LEASING – See Chapter 9, #13 "Foolproof Lease Verification Formula." This is the best way to verify your monthly lease payment and total-due-at-lease-signing quoted to you by the dealer.

CASH PURCHASE or FINANCE use the calling guide below:

Ask the dealer:
    1. "What is the total out-the-door price of the car?"
Then ask:
    2. "What's the price breakdown that brings you to this total?"
Enter the figures on their appropriate line. Price breakdown includes items such as:

Price of car _____
Sales tax_____
License fee_____
Tire fee_____
Document fee_____ (dealership paperwork fee)
Other _____ (any item that contributes to the total price)
Other _____
Total _____

Have the dealer explain any item you may not understand. Make sure they don't include dealer prep and advertising fees (this rarely happens). If they do include them, try to get them deleted and if they won't, call another dealer or two to see if they will sell you a car without those fees.

FINANCING (only) — Ask the dealer:

    1. "How much is the down payment?" _____ (or *you* decide how much you want to put down)
    2. "Is the first monthly payment included in the down payment?"
Yes No
    3. "After I pay the down payment, how many days until my next monthly payment is due?" _____ (example: 30, 45, 90 days etc.)
    4. "How much is the monthly payment?" _____
    5. "How many monthly payments remain after the down payment?"

_____

6. "What is the interest rate?" _____%

7. "What is my total out of pocket from down payment to final monthly payment?" _____ (optional)

Caution: Make sure the dealership will accept a check from your loan source (call and ask the finance manager). At the last minute, they could say: "Oh, you're paying with an (for example) onlineloan.com check? We don't accept those checks but we can finance you!" (for a higher rate of course)

☞ See "Loan Interest Table" in the Appendix or the following websites for a calculator that will help you verify the dealer's quoted finance numbers:

www.autovantage.com   5★
Click on **Car Research** then under "Finance Tools", click on **Loan Calculator**

www.autoweb.com   5★
Scroll to "Financing & Research" and click on **Auto Loan Calculator**

www.carpoint.msn.com   5★
On left side, click on **Finance**

www.eloan.com   5★
Click on **Auto Purchase** then on right side, click on **Rates and Payments**

5- Credit Check Pitfalls

The dealership usually insists on a credit check, regardless of whether you finance, lease, pay with cash or a cashier's check. Doing it by fax will save you from:

➤ Having to wait up to two hours in a busy dealership going through their credit check process.

➤ A face-to-face encounter with the finance manager who will attempt to raise your interest rate.

Ask the dealer, before you go in to pick up the car, if they need to run your credit check.

Caution: Misrepresenting information on your credit application can come back at you with possible penalties if the deal has already been consummated.

6- How to Get Your Credit Checked

Personal information typically asked on a credit application may include: social security number, sources of income, how long you've been working at your job, verifiable income, dependents, how long you've been living where you are, your home phone number, how much you pay for rent, other monthly financial obligations, names, addresses and phone numbers of three personal references.

♦ **You may be asked for proof of income such as two current pay stubs or recent tax return.**

Have your contact person fax you a credit application. Make sure they write their 'return fax number' and 'attention to' name on the front of the application so you don't have to call them later asking for this information. Fill it out, sign it, write attention to whom and fax it back.

♦ **If you don't own a fax machine, have the dealer overnight the credit application fill it out and send it back.**

Caution: Have your credit checked only once and that's with the dealer you get your car from. Having it checked with more than one dealer in a short period of a week or two can lower your credit rating. This means you may be charged a higher interest rate on your final deal. If needed, talk to a loan officer at your bank for more details.

After you fax it, call and ask your contact person:

1. "Could you check to see if my fax went through? I'll hold the line while you check."

They'll say: "Sure" and then they'll go and check.

When they return to tell you it's there, ask:

2. "How long will it take to run the credit check?"

They may say: "30 minutes." (It varies between 15 minutes to 2 hours depending on how busy they are.)

You reply:

3. If you want to keep things moving along, say: "Okay, I'll call you back in 30 minutes." (or you can wait for them to call you)

If you call them back in 30 minutes, say:

4. "Did you have a chance to run my credit check?"
If they say: "no," ask: "How long before you can have it done?"
If they say: "yes," ask: "How does it look?"

If it looks good, confirm that the interest rate is what you previously agreed to.

If they say there are some glitches, you will have to renegotiate your interest rate. Keep in mind you're on the phone which puts you in a much better negotiating position than if you were in the dealership and at their mercy. Whatever rate they ask for, negotiate at least two points off. If they are not agreeable with that, see if they'll come down at all. If not, you might want to call your bank or credit union.

7- Your Trade-In

Now is the best time to discuss your trade-in by phone. If you haven't figured out your trade-in value by now, read Chapter 5: "Your Trade-in's value." Ask your contact person what they will offer you for your car. They usually say they can't make an offer until they see the car. Tell them that if your description of the car is inaccurate, you understand that the price will be reduced appropriately.

Caution: When you sell your trade-in to a dealer, make sure you sign an Odometer Disclosure Statement at the dealership with your vehicle's actual miles clearly identified. If someone were to roll back the miles before the car was re-sold, you would be the liable party, not the dealer. Sign the Odometer Disclosure Statement only after the miles are written or typed onto the sheet that you sign.

If you are trading-in your car, you'll need to have the title with you.

If it's been lost, don't worry about it. The dealer will have you sign a lost title form and that'll be the end of that.

If you have credit life/disability insurance and/or an extended warranty policy on your trade-in, a prorated refund may be in order upon early cancellation. Call the appropriate company to ask if a refund is available, how much it is and when you can expect to get it. This refund may go toward your down payment or you can collect it from the dealer at a later date. If the refund will be mailed to the dealership, make sure you check back from time to time to ensure your collection of this refund.

8- Your Contact Person

You are now ready to make an appointment to pick up your new car or have it delivered to you.

If your contact person cannot be present when you pick up the car, ask who your new contact person will be.

Call this new contact person and go over all the details of your transaction and make sure you are in agreement on every point.

The dealership will need to photocopy your driver's license and current insurance card. Be sure to have these and a check with you when you go in.

You should pick up your new car the same day you finalize negotiations. Unless the dealer accepted a deposit, the price you negotiated is most likely so low that a walk-in customer could potentially buy the car from a salesperson for more money.

You might be able to get the dealer to deliver the car to you. Ask the dealer: "Will you deliver the car with the contract to my home (or office)?" If they deliver the car, still follow the steps in the next chapter.

13

Looking Over Your New Car... and Paperwork

In This Chapter
1- Due Bill (what the dealer still owes you)
2- Final Paperwork

Here are some details you should be aware of when finalizing your transaction. Once at the dealership, find your contact person and ask to see the car. Look over the Monroney Sticker which is typically on one of the side windows. It identifies the car by Vehicle Identification Number (VIN), year, make, model, color, options, packages, standard features, includes the Manufacturer's Suggested Retail Price (MSRP) and every detail that make up that vehicle. It is also known as the window sticker.

If the car is being delivered to you, you'll want to look over the window sticker verifying the information is the same as you were given over the phone and/or fax. If you want, match the VIN on the window sticker to the one on the car by looking through the driver's side windshield or on the driver's door jamb. You should keep the window sticker as it is helpful to have on hand when you re-sell the car.

Did the dealer:

- ➤ detail the car?

- ➤ fill the gas tank?

- ➤ put in a set of mats?

> ➤ do everything else they agreed to?

Verify the mileage on the odometer and take your vehicle for a test drive if you would like.

Make sure you are not being charged for an accessory you did not ask for. Don't let them pressure you into paying for it, have it removed.

Inspect the car for any possible damage. Walk around the car slowly and look at every panel (including the undercarriage) for scratches, nicks and problems new cars should not have. You can do the same with the interior, engine bay and trunk if you want. If it is raining, ask to have it dried and look at it in a dry area. Rain can hide minor damage.

If you find any damage, you can have the dealer fix it before you sign the contract. But most likely, you'll buy the car and have the repairs done later. Make sure you put the repairs in writing on the Due Bill (see below). It should read something like: The 'front right panel' will be repaired to the customer's satisfaction. Also, you want the Due Bill to specify that a free loaner car will be supplied for the duration of repairs.

1- Due Bill (What the dealer still owes you)

The Due Bill can be called by other similar names at times (example: IOU). It is a typed agreement for items or repairs promised to you at a future date by the dealership.

These items will be delivered, installed or repaired after you buy or lease your car. Try to have a loaner car available when you drop off your new car for agreed work. Have them write it on the Due Bill, 'Loaner Car.'

For example: If you want a roof rack and the parts department is out of stock, this item will go on the Due Bill to be installed at a later date.

Dealers usually won't install add-on items before a car is sold because customers change their minds at the last minute and the dealer doesn't want to be stuck with a customized car.

2- Final Paperwork

Once in the finance room, relax while you look over the paperwork. Staying focused and not allowing yourself to be pressured is best when looking over your contract.

There will be numerous pieces of paper you will be signing (insurance, Due Bill, etc.). Look over this paperwork slowly and when you are ready, sign where needed. If you have any questions, ask the finance manager to explain to your satisfaction before you sign.

If you need to have paperwork redone, read the fresh one as if you were reading it for the first time. Pay attention to all the points, not only the changed item.

When the contract is in front of you, ask the finance manager: "Is this the final paperwork requiring my signature?" If there is further paperwork, say: "I would like to sign that paperwork before I sign the contract." The contract should be the last document you sign. Signing the contract last assures the dealer cannot renege on any other portion of your agreed-upon deal.

When you get to the contract, read all the typed-in information carefully comparing them to your notes. If you don't pay attention, do not expect the manufacturer to bail you out later if you feel the dealer was unfair.

If you are purchasing the vehicle, make sure it is a purchase contract and not a lease contract. It will say one of the following at the top of the contract: Purchase, Finance or Lease.

You wouldn't want to go home with your new car, reread the contract in the relaxed comfort of your home and find that you just leased a car when you thought you bought it.

If the car is new, the contract must state the word "new," not "used," "demo" or "pre-owned."

If you have a trade-in, make sure it is specified in the contract.

Make sure you leave with an easily readable copy of the contract, Due Bill and any other paperwork you signed or were given.

Fortunately, most new vehicle inspections and paperwork are problem-free.

Congratulations on your new automobile!

14

Online Information and Buying Services

This Internet Directory includes every website necessary to purchase or lease a new car easily and for the lowest price.

STAR RATINGS: Hundreds of hours were spent sifting through hundreds of websites to obtain the best information each site had to offer. The information on most of these websites was given a star rating by the author. Only 4 to 5 star information from any given website (5 being best) is included in this directory.

If you decide to buy or lease through an Online Car-Buying Service, make sure to read Chapter 12, "Finalizing the Deal." It offers important guidelines you should know before stepping foot on the dealers lot.

♦ Websites change format periodically. If an instruction given in this Directory is no longer valid, the information you want is probably still on the website. Proceed using your best judgment.

Some manufacturers (such as Ford and GMC) offer dealer inventory and window sticker information for specific vehicles. (For example, you could go to www.ford.com, click on the 'Ford' logo; then click on 'view dealer inventory' and follow the instructions to the model of choice.) Most manufacturers do not offer dealer inventory online at this time.

Disclaimer: The author assumes no liability for security or privacy difficulties that may arise due to information you disclose on the Internet.

Internet Directory

Researching Your Next Car

Car Reviews

Safety Data and Recalls

You Might Want to Know...

New Car Specifications & Pricing

Dealer Phone Numbers, Websites and More

Warranty Information

Insurance Information

Cutting-Edge Information

Manufacturers' Contact Information

1. Deciding What Type of Car You Want

www.autobytel.com   4.5★

www.cars.com (also recycler.com) 4★

www.carsdirect.com   4.5★

www.jdpower.com   5★
Click on **Automotive** then **Help me choose**

www.kbb.com   4.5★
(Kelley Blue Book site)

www.motortrend.com   4★

2. Photo Gallery of New Cars

Also see manufacturers' site (#42 in this directory)

www.autobytel.com   5★

www.autosite.com   5★

www.carsdirect.com   4★

For photo viewing of "Concept Cars", go to #40 in this directory

3. 360 Degree Viewing of Interior & Exterior

Also see manufacturers' site (#42 in this directory)

www.cars.com (also recycler.com) 4.5★
Click on **Research** then click on **"360 Interior Views"**

www.autos.msn.com   5★

4. All Manufacturers' Models at a Glance

www.autosite.com   5★

www.vehix.com   5★

5. Available Model Colors

Also see manufacturers' site (#42 in this directory)

www.carsdirect.com   4.5★
Select a **Make** and **Model**

www.carprices.com   5★
Click on **Build & Price Your Car**

www.edmunds.com   4★
Click on **New Cars**

6. Choose a Model, Then View Its Competitors

www.autosite.com   4★
Click on **New Cars**

www.edmunds.com   5★
Click on **New Cars**

7. Side- by-Side Car Comparison

www.autos.msn.com   5★
Click on **New Cars**

www.carsdirect.com   5★
Click on **Make**, **Model** and **Go**

8. Previews of New Car Body Styles

www.cars.com (also recycler.com)   5★
Click on **Research** then click on **All New Models for "current year"**

www.kbb.com   5★
Under "NEW CAR REVIEWS" click on **Coming soon**

www.edmunds.com   5★
Click on **Car Reviews** then click on **Future Vehicles**

9. Best Selling Models

www.autobytel.com   5★
Click on **Research** then "Top 10"

www.carprices.com   5★
Click on **Top Ten Lists**

10. Reviews by the Experts

Future and concept cars are under item #**40** in this directory

www.automobilemag.com   4★

www.carpoint.msn.com   4★
Click on **New Cars** then click on **Reviews**

www.caranddriver.com   4.5★

www.carsmart.com   4★
Under "Car Research", click on **Reviews**

www.edmunds.com   4.5★
Click on **Car Reviews**

www.motortrend.com   5★
Under "Road Tests" click on your "vehicle style"

New Car Test Drive
www.nctd.com   4.5★
Current and past test drive reviews

www.thecarconnection.com   4★
Click on **Reviews**

www.roadandtrack.com   5★

11. Auto Experts Favorite Car Choices

www.edmunds.com   4.5★
Click on **CAR REVIEWS** then click on **Editors' Most Wanted**

12. Crash / Injury / Theft Data

Insurance Institute for Highway Safety
www.hwysafety.org   5★
Click on **Vehicle Ratings**

National Highway Traffic Safety Administration
www.nhtsa.dot.gov   4.5★
Click on **Crash Tests**

Theft
www.cars.com (also recycler.com)5★
Click on **Advice** then click on **Top Theft Target**

13. Manufacturers' Recalls (example: Firestone tires)

Recall information can help give you an idea how well a vehicle
is built.

www.alldata.com   5★
Click on **Recalls & Technical Service Bulletins**

www.autoweb.com   4★
Click on **Research New Vehicles** then click on **Recalls**

National Highway Traffic Safety Administration
www.nhtsa.dot.gov   5★
Click on **Recalls**

14. Actual Location Where a Car Is Built

www.autosite.com   5★
Click on **Research** then choose a "Make" and "Model", click on
Tech Specs then click on **Where Built**

15. What This New Car Will Cost You Over 5 Years

www.intellichoice.com
Click on **Research New Cars**, choose a **Make** then click on
Ownership cost

16. New Car Specifications / Packages / Options/ Pricing (BUYING SERVICES)

The following Online Car Buying Services offer detailed information on specifications, packages, options and pricing. If you decide to buy or lease a car through one of these Online Car Buying Services, a contact person from a local dealership will call you, usually within twenty-four hours. Be prepared, read Chapter 12, "Finalizing the Deal," and ask the necessary questions while on the phone. There are numerous ways that a dealer can still make huge profits from your deal in the finance room. Chapter 12 shows you how to keep further dealer profits in your pocket.

Getting a quote through an Online Car Buying Service is free and there are no obligations to buy. Although they will offer you a good price, if getting the absolute lowest price is your main priority, see Chapter 11, "Locate and Negotiate By Phone."

www.autobytel.com   4.3★
Click on **Research**, choose a "Make"

www.autosite.com   4.8★
Click on **Research**, choose a "Make"

www.autovantage.com   4.4★
Under "Car research", click on **New car summaries**

www.autoweb.com   4★
Under "Research", click on **New vehicles**

www.carpoint.com   4.8★
Choose a **Make** and **Model.** Clicking on an **option box** will update your total at bottom right

www.carprices.com   4.5★
Click on **Build & Price Your Car**

www.cars.com   5★
Choose a "Make", "Model" enter "Zip code" and click on **Price with options**

www.carsdirect.com   5★
Select a **Make, Model** and click on **Go**

www.edmunds.com   4.8★
Click on **New cars**

www.kbb.com   4.5★
Click on **New car pricing**

www.motortrend.com   4.9★
Click on **New Vehicle Prices/Reports**. Includes manufacturer codes for options/packages

The manufacturers' site (#42 in this directory) will help you with vehicle specific information but is not an Online Car Buying Service.

17. View Bargain Prices You Can Offer a Dealer

Target prices to base an offer on
www.intellichoice.com   4.9★
Click on **New Models**

www.carsdirect.com   4.9★
Choose a "Make", "Model" and click **GO**

Actual negotiated car prices (updated weekly)
www.edmunds.com   4.7★
Click on **NEW CARS** to find True Market Value

www.stoneage.com   5★
Click on **Research**

18. Leasing & Buying Information

www.autopedia.com   4.5★
Scroll and click on **Financing and Leasing Information**

www.bankrate.com   4.5★
Click on **Auto Loans**

19. Buyers' Frequently Asked Questions

www.edmunds.com   5★
Click on **Tips & Advice**, scroll to "Keyword Search", type in **car buying**

20. Specific Information about Leasing

www.alg.com   5★
Click on **News & Information**

www.carwizard.com   5★
Click on **Leasing**

www.leasesource.com   5★
Click any menu heading

www.autoleasingsoftware.com
For a fee, this program will help you calculate your lease

21. Can I Afford My Dream Car? (Instant Quotes)

www.carsdirect.com   5★
Select your **"Make"** and "Model" then under "We Have Great Low
Rates", click on **Learn more**

22. Your Budget vs. Monthly Payments

www.autovantage.com   5★
Click on **Car Research** then under "Finance Tools", click on **Loan
Calculator**

www.autoweb.com   5★
Scroll to "Financing & Research" and click on **Auto Loan
Calculator**

www.carpoint.msn.com   5★
On left side, click on **Finance**

www.eloan.com   5★
Click on **Auto Purchase** then on right side, click on **Rates and
Payments**

23. Compare Loan / Lease Payments Easily

www.leasesource.com   5★
Click on **Lease Workshop** then click on **Run the Numbers**

24. What the Credit Agencies Look at to Rate You

www.bankrate.com   5★

Click on **Auto Loans** then click on **Checking Your Credit** then click on any "Link" for a well rounded view of how credit ratings work and the interest rate you can expect to pay

www.eloan.com   5★

Explains: credit scoring, what lenders consider, how to improve your score, how to contact credit bureaus with issues

Click on **Auto Purchase** then on right side, click on **Free credit report** then under "Free Credit Report", click on **View Sample**

www.ficoguide.com   5★

Click on "Link" of choice under **Credit Education**

25. Get Your Own Credit Report Fast

www.creditreport.com

Get your personal credit report mailed to you in 1 to 5 days for a fee

www.equifax.com

Order your credit report sent to your e-mail address for a fee

www.ficoguide.com

www.mycreditfile.com

www.qspace.com

Explains credit scores. See your credit report online in seconds and it won't show as an inquiry

www.transunion.com

Order and view online

26. Frequently Asked Questions about Getting a Loan

www.eloan.com

Click on **Auto Purchase** then on menu bar below, click on **FAQ's** for information on loan acquisitions. Very informative

27. View Interest Rates & Obtain a Loan

Check with your dealership's finance department to make sure they will accept a check from any of the following loan sources.

Caution: Before sending private information to any website, you may want to ask if they will forward your information to any source other than their own company.

www.bankrate.com
Click on **Auto Loans**

www.capitolone.com

www.eloan.com
Click on **Auto Purchase** to view interest rates for excellent to poor credit ratings

www.peoplefirst.com
User friendly site for people with good credit

www.virtualbank.com
Go to "Lending Center" then "Auto" and click on **New – Dealer.** View interest rates and monthly payments instantly

28. Poor Credit? ...Get a Loan Here

www.carloan.com

www.carsdirect.com
Select your "Make" and "Model" then click on **Got Bad Credit?**

www.householdauto.com
Click on **Less than perfect credit?**

29. Used Car Book Values

www.kbb.com   5★
Click on **Trade-In Value** or **Private Party Value**

www.nadaguides.com   5★
Click on **Automobiles**

30. Classified Listings for Price Comparisons

www.autotrader.com   5★

www.cars.com   4.5★

31. Rebates & Incentives

The following websites are updated on varying schedules. It's best to look at every site to see how many have similar prices.

www.autobytel.com   4★
Click on **Research**

www.autopedia.com   4★
Scroll and click on **Consumer incentives and rebates**

www.autosite.com   5★
Click on **Research**

www.edmunds.com   5★
Click on **Incentives and Rebates**

www.intellichoice.com   4.5★
Scroll and click on **Rebates and Incentives**

www.kbb.com   5★

32. Factory to Dealer Holdback (dealer's hidden profit)

Factory to dealer holdback is a percentage of a vehicle's price paid to the dealer by the manufacturer (not an incentive).

www.edmunds.com   5★
Scroll and click on **Dealer Holdback**

33. Dealer Locator & Maps

Also see manufacturers' site (#42 in this directory)

www.cars.com   4.5★
Click on **Find A Car Dealer Near You**

34. Dealer's Inventory (not a complete list)

Also see manufacturers' site (#42 in this directory)

www.dealernet.com   4★
Click on "Quick Jump" pull down menu **arrow** and click on
Inventory search

35. All Manufacturers' Warranties at Glance

www.cars.com   5★
Scroll and click on **Advice** then click on **Warranty Comparison**

36. The Extended Warranty & Your Rights

Federal Trade Commission
www.ftc.gov
This site will give you tips on what to ask, what to watch for and
what your rights are before you buy an extended warranty.
In the Site Map "search box" on top right, type in "Auto Service
Contract Rights" and click on **GO**

37. Extended Warranty Quotes & Information

See Chapter 8, "The Extended Warranty" for information on what
to look for and what to ask.

www.1sourceautowarranty.com
View prices instantly and an actual contract

www.carsdirect.com
Click on **Extended Warranties**

www.certifiedcarcare.com
User friendly site. Click on **Instant Quote Click Here**

www.warrantydirect.com

www.warrantygold.com

38. Frequently Asked Questions About Insurance

www.geico.com
Click on **Auto Insurance** then click on **Your auto insurance coverage explained**

www.faqfarm.com
Click on **Car Insurance**

www.insure.com
Scroll to "Have a question?" and click on **Auto Insurance FAQ**

39. Instant Insurance Price Quotes

To get an insurance price quote at any of these sites, have your current policy available.

www.autobytel.com
Click on **New** then scroll and click on **Insurance tools and research**

www.esurance.com
Enter "Zip Code", click **go** and fill-in a 5 to 7 minute form to get an instant quote

www.insure.com
Click on **Auto**

40. Fun / Exciting / Informative Websites

Concept Cars

www.kbb.com
Under the heading "New Car Reviews & Ratings", click on **coming soon**

www.edmunds.com
Scroll to click on **Car Reviews** then click on **Concept Cars**

Next Years Changes & New Entries

www.cars.com
Click on **All-New Models for 2004** (or 2005)

www.edmunds.com
Scroll to click on **Car Reviews** then click on **Future Vehicles**

www.motortrend.com
Click on **future vehicles** (covers 1 to 4 future years)

Automotive Encyclopedia

www.autopedia.com
Scroll and click on anything of interest

Miles Per Gallon

www.cars.com
Scroll and click on **Advice** then under "Top 10's" click on "link" of choice

Hybrid/Fuel Economy

http://epa.gov/greenvehicles/

www.fueleconomy.gov

www.greencar.com

www.motortrend.com
On left side, click on **Alternative/Hybrid**

News

www.auto.com
Daily news, auto shows

www.autonews.com

www.autoweek.com

www.motortrend.com
Click on **Auto News**

Aftermarket Wheels

www.tirerack.com

Number of Vehicles Sold Per Manufacturer
www.autosite.com
Scroll and click on **Market Report**

Chat Room
www.edmunds.com
Scroll and click on **Town Hall Discussions**

Lemon Law
www.autopedia.com
If you have an ongoing problem with your new vehicle and it's out of service for a period of time, it could be a lemon. This site explains the lemon law for all 50 states and how to get legal help. Click on **Got a Lemon? Get AUTOPEDIA'S 4 Star Award winning Lemonaid!** then click on LEMON then scroll and click on your **State**

41. Websites With Links to Manufacturers' Websites and 800 Phone Numbers

www.autopedia.com
Scroll past list of links and under the heading **Auto Manufacturers**, click on **800 Phone Numbers**

www.jdpower.com
Click on **Automotive** then click on **Link to a manufacturer**. View 800 numbers too

www.kbb.com
Sites only. Click on the heading **Tools, Tips, Advice** then scroll to bottom and click on **manufacturer**

42. List of Manufacturer's Website Addresses

These manufacturer's websites offer vehicle information, dealership locations and phone numbers. Some manufacturers (such as Ford and GMC) offer current dealer inventory and window sticker information for specific vehicles. (For example, you would find a Ford Explorer by first going to www.ford.com, clicking on the 'Ford' logo; then on 'view dealer inventory' and following the instructions given.) Not all manufacturers offer dealer inventory at this time.

www.acura.com
www.alfaromeo.com
www.astonmartin.com
www.audiusa.com
www.bentleymotors.co.uk
www.bmwusa.com
www.buick.com
www.cadillac.com
www.chevrolet.com
www.chrysler.com
www.daewoous.com
www.dodge.com
www.ferrari.com
www.ford.com
www.fordvehicles.com
www.gmev.com (GM EV1)
www.gmc.com
www.gmbuypower.com
www.honda.com
www.hummer.com
www.hyundaiusa.com
www.infiniti.com
www.isuzu.com
www.jaguar.com/us
www.jeep.com

www.kia.com
www.lamborghini.com
www.landrover.com
www.lexus.com
www.lexussafety.com
www.lincoln.com
www.lotuscars.com
www.mazdausa.com
www.mbusa.com (Mercedes)
www.mercuryvehicles.com
www.miniusa.com
www.mitsubishicars.com
www.nissanusa.com
www.oldsmobile.com
www.pontiac.com
www.porsche.com
www.saabusa.com
www.saturn.com
www.scion.com
www.subaru.com
www.suzuki.com
www.suzukiauto.com
www.toyota.com
www.vw.com
www.volvocars.com

Appendix

In This Section

Loan Interest Table
Manufacturer's Consumer Hotline Numbers
Manufacturer's Warranty Chart

Loan Interest Table Explained

1. Locate your interest rate in the left column, then your loan term (number of months) in the top row.

2. Multiply the amount at the intersection of the interest rate and loan term by the number of thousands borrowed.

Example: Say you are borrowing $10,000 on a 60 month loan at 5%. Multiply the intersection amount of $18.87 by 10 ($10,000) which equals a monthly payment of $188.70.

Loan Interest Table

Approximate Monthly Payment Per $1,000 Borrowed

Loan Term	12	24	36	48	60	72	84	96
% Rate								
0%	83.33	41.66	27.7	20.83	16.66	13.88	11.90	10.41
1%	83.78	42.10	28.20	21.26	17.09	14.31	12.33	10.84
2%	84.23	42.54	28.64	21.69	17.52	14.75	12.76	11.28
3%	84.69	42.98	29.08	22.13	17.96	15.19	13.21	11.72
4%	85.14	43.42	29.52	22.57	18.41	15.64	13.66	12.18
5%	85.60	43.87	29.97	23.02	18.87	16.10	14.13	12.65
6%	86.06	44.32	30.42	23.50	19.33	16.57	14.60	13.14
7%	86.52	44.77	30.87	23.94	19.80	17.04	15.09	13.63
8%	86.98	45.22	31.33	24.41	20.27	17.53	15.58	14.13
9%	87.45	45.68	31.79	24.88	20.75	18.02	16.08	14.65
10%	87.91	46.14	32.26	25.36	21.24	18.52	16.60	15.17
11%	88.38	46.60	32.73	25.84	21.74	19.03	17.12	15.70
12%	88.84	47.07	33.21	26.33	22.24	19.55	17.65	16.25
13%	89.31	47.54	33.69	26.82	22.75	20.07	18.19	16.80
14%	89.78	48.01	34.17	27.32	23.26	20.60	18.74	17.37
15%	90.25	48.48	34.66	27.83	23.80	21.14	19.29	17.94
16%	90.73	48.96	35.15	28.34	24.31	21.69	19.86	18.52
17%	91.20	49.44	35.65	28.85	24.85	22.24	20.43	19.12
18%	91.67	49.92	36.15	29.37	25.39	22.80	21.01	19.72
19%	92.15	50.40	36.65	29.90	25.94	23.37	21.60	20.33
20%	92.63	50.89	37.16	30.43	26.49	23.95	22.20	20.95
21%	93.11	51.38	37.67	30.96	27.05	24.53	22.81	21.58
22%	93.59	51.87	38.19	31.50	27.61	25.12	23.42	22.21
23%	94.07	52.37	38.70	32.05	28.19	25.72	24.04	22.86

Tip: A 1% increase adds $300 to a 60 month loan per $10,000 borrowed

Manufacturer's Consumer Hotline Numbers

Acura	(800)382-2238	Lexus	(800)255-3987
Audi	(800)822-2834	Lincoln	(800)392-3673
Bentley	(248)340-6464	Mazda	(800)222-5500
BMW	(800)831-1117	Mercedes-Benz	(800)222-0100
Buick	(800)521-7300	Mercury	(800)392-3673
Cadillac	(800)458-8006	Mini	(866)275-6464
Chevrolet	(800)222-1020	Mitsubishi	(800)222-0037
Chrysler	(800)247-9753	Nissan	(800)647-7261
Daewoo	(877)463-2396	Oldsmobile	(800)442-6537
Dodge	(800)423-6343	Plymouth	(800)759-6688
Ferrari	(201)816-2600	Pontiac	(800)762-2737
Ford	(800)392-3673	Porsche	(800)545-8039
GM EV1	(888) 382-7747	Rolls Royce	(248)340-6464
GM	(800)462-8782	Saab	(800)955-9007
Honda	(800)999-1009	Saturn	(800)553-6000
Hummer	(800)348-6833	Subaru	(800)782-2783
Hyundai	(800)633-5151	Suzuki	(800)934-0934
Infiniti	(800)662-6200	Toyota	(800)331-4331
Isuzu	(800)255-6727	Volkswagen	(800)822-8987
Jaguar	(800)452-4827	Volvo	(800)458-1552
Jeep	(800)925-5337		
Kia	(800)333-4542		
Land Rover	(800)346-3493		

If a number is invalid, call a dealer for the current number.

Manufacturer's Warranty Chart

Make	Bumper-to-Bumper years / miles	Free Scheduled Maintenance years / miles	Drivetrain years / miles	Rust/ Corrosion years / miles	Roadside Assistance years / miles
Acura	4 50,000	none	4 50,000	5 Unlimited*	4 50,000
Audi	4 50,000	4 50,000	4 50,000	12 Unlimited*	4 50,000
BMW	4 50,000	4 50,000	4 50,000	6 Unlimited*	4 50,000
Buick	3 36,000	none	3 36,000	6 100,000	3 36,000
Cadillac	4 50,000	none	4 50,000	6 100,000	4 50,000
Chevrolet	3 36,000	none	3 36,000	6 100,000	3 36,000
Chrysler	3 36,000	none	7 70,000	5 100,000	3 36,000
Daewoo	3 36,000	none	5 60,000	5 Unlimited*	3 36,000
Dodge	3 36,000	none	7 70,000	5 100,000	3 36,000
Ford	3 36,000	none	3 36,000	5 Unlimited*	3 36,000
GMC	3 36,000	none	3 36,000	6 100,000	3 36,000
Honda	3 36,000	none	3 36,000	5 Unlimited*	none
Hummer	3 36,000	none	3 36,000	6 100,000	none
Hyundai	5 60,000	none	10 100,000	5 100,000	5 Unlimited*
Infiniti	4 60,000	none	6 70,000	7 Unlimited*	4 Unlimited*
Isuzu	3 50,000	none	10 120,000	6 100,000	5 60,000
Jaguar	4 50,000	4 50,000	4 50,000	6 Unlimited*	4 50,000
Jeep	3 36,000	none	7 70,000	5 100,00	3 36,000
Kia	5 60,000	none	10 100,000	5 100,000	5 100,000
Land Rover	4 50,000	4 50,000**	4 50,000	6 Unlimited*	4 50,000
Lexus	4 50,000	5,000	6 70,000	6 Unlimited*	4 Unlimited*
Lincoln	4 50,000	1 12,000	4 50,000	5 Unlimited*	4 50,000
Mazda	3 50,000	none	3 50,000	5 Unlimited*	3 50,000
Mercedes	4 50,000	4 50,000	4 50,000	4 50,000	Unlimited*
Mercury	3 36,000	none	3 36,000	5 Unlimited	3 36,000
Mini	4 50,000	3 36,000	4 50,000	6 Unlimited	4 50,000
Mitsubishi	3 36,000	none	5 60,000	7 100,000	3 36,000
Nissan	3 36,000	none	5 60,000	5 Unlimited	none
Oldsmobile	3 36,000	none	3 36,000	6 100,000	3 36,000
Pontiac	3 36,000	none	3 36,000	6 100,000	3 36,000
Porsche	4 50,000	none	4 50,000	10 Unlimited*	4 50,000
Saab	4 50,000	3 36,000	4 50,000	6 Unlimited*	4 50,000
Saturn	3 36,000	none	3 36,000	6 100,000	3 36,000
Subaru	3 36,000	none	5 60,000	5 Unlimited*	3 36,000
Suzuki	3 36,000	none	7 100,000	3 Unlimited*	none
Toyota/Scion	3 36,000	none	5 60,000	5 Unlimited*	none
Volkswagen	4 50,000	none	5 60,000	12 Unlimited*	2 Unlimited*
Volvo	4 50,000	3 30,000	4 50,000	8 Unlimited*	4 Unlimited*

*No mileage limit within the time frame (years) allotted. **Does not apply on Freelander.
For current warranty information go to **www.cars.com** or the manufacturer's website.

Index

Your opinion about this book matters!

Send an e-mail to: <u>a.sb@verizon.net</u>

Or send a note to:

Quickread Publishing
P.O. Box 213
Santa Barbara, CA 93102

To order:

Top Secrets Revealed
The Hassle Free Approach To
Car Buying & Leasing

ISBN: 0-9748947-0-2

Call: (805) 682-6787
We accept Visa, Mastercard
American Express and Discover

or

E-mail: events@chaucersbooks.com

or go to:

www.amazingcardeals.com